D1441233

Local Area Networks

WILEY SERIES IN COMPUTING

Consulting Editor
Professor D. W. Barron
*Computer Studies Group, Southampton University,
Southampton, England*

Local Area Networks
Issues, Products, and Developments

V. E. Cheong

Scicon Consultancy Ltd.
London, England

and

R. A. Hirschheim

London School of Economics
London, England

A Wiley–Interscience Publication

JOHN WILEY & SONS
Chichester · New York · Brisbane · Toronto · Singapore

Library of Congress Cataloging in Publication Data:

Cheong, V. E. (Viv E.)
  Local area networks.
  (Wiley series in computing)
  Bibliography: P.
  Includes index.
  1. Office practice—Automation. 2. Information networks. I. Hirschheim, R. A. (Rudy A.) II. Title. III. Series.
HF5547.5.C485   1983   651.8'4404   82-23778
ISBN 0 471 90134 2

British Library Cataloguing in Publication Data:

Cheong, V. E.
  Local area networks—(Wiley series in computing)
  1. Computers networks.
I. Title. II. Hirschheim, R.A.
001.64'404   TK5105.5
ISBN 0 471 90134 2

Printed by Whitefriars Press Ltd, Tonbridge, Kent

To Jane and Sally

Contents

PART II: Products, Evaluation, and Developments

PART III: Appendices

Preface

Local area networks (LANs) have aroused a good deal of interest in the last few years because of their potential role in the area of office automation. LANs provide the facility through which the various technologies of the automated office communicate with one another. Yet much of the enthusiasm for LANs comes from what they purport to do rather than what the available products actually do. And there is more than just a little confusion surrounding local area networks.

This text attempts to allay this confusion by synthesizing a number of the important concepts, issues, and approaches put forward by various LAN proponents. In doing so, it is hoped that the reader will become familiar with what local area networks are and what they do, as well as the potential contribution that they may make to the automated office.

The text is divided into two parts: the first somewhat more academic and tutorial in nature, the second more practical and implementation oriented. Part I, entitled 'Concepts, Capabilities, and Comparisons', lays the groundwork for discussing what LANs are, what they are capable of doing (and not doing), how they can be classified, and so on. Part I also presents a comparison of two major LANs: the Cambridge Ring and the Ethernet. Part II, entitled 'Products, Evaluation, and Developments', offers a description of the more common LAN products along with some criteria upon which to evaluate them. Organizational and implementation issues are also treated in this part.

To describe the text in more detail, Part I contains five chapters. The first chapter attempts to define LANs by drawing together those characteristics of LANs which are most generally cited by the various authors who have attempted to define them in the past. This chapter intends to inform the reader of some of the attributes of LANs which distinguish them from wide area networks (WANs). It is noteworthy, however, that due to the recency of the technology there is no internationally agreed definition of a LAN.

Chapter 2 discusses the causal factors which have led to the development of LANs. It highlights the degradation in relative cost/performance of WANs and the technological advances that have accompanied the developments and maturing of the automated office concepts as well as the trend towards distributed processing. The close proximity of the majority of office communication channels means that LANs can employ simple topologies and control strategies which have been designed and developed to solve local problems.

Chapter 3 considers the capabilities that LANs offer, as well as what they ought to offer any prospective user. Technical requirements such as high data rates, low error rates, and protocol simplicity are among such LAN characteristics. Yet non-technical characteristics need attention as well; in fact, office environments might demand that non-technical aspects take precedence over the technical ones.

Chapter 4 concerns itself with the various classes of LANs. Drawing upon the taxonomies of a number of authors, this chapter puts forward a classification scheme by which to classify LANs based on topologies and control strategies.

Chapter 5 concentrates on a comparison of two major LANs: the Cambridge Ring and the Ethernet. Unfortunately, owing to the limited and often contradictory evidence available on issues such as performance, reliability, and the like, this chapter makes no definitive statement about the superiority of one approach over the other.

Part II also contains five chapters, but its subject matter may be considered to be more practically oriented in nature. Chapter 6 describes a number of LAN products. It must be borne in mind that the products chosen for inclusion in this chapter are those products for which there is relatively easy access to product descriptions and other relevant material at the present time. The LAN products chosen are felt to be representative of what is available on the market. It must be stressed, however, that the number of LANs being offered by different vendors is growing rapidly. Thus, what might be representative today may change in the future.

Chapter 7 introduces a number of other factors that may be relevant when attempting to evaluate LANs. These include such issues as: transmission media, maintenance, security, integrity, extensibility, and so on.

Chapter 8 looks at some future developments which might have a marked effect on LANs. These future developments seem important as they have the potential for dramatically altering what LANs do and the way they do it. Key topics covered in this chapter are high- level protocols and LAN standards. Other issues addressed in this chapter are: the development of the 'super-intelligent' terminal, LAN-LAN and LAN-WAN interconnection, and legal aspects of LANs.

Chapters 9 and 10 are very much more organizational in nature and attempt to look at the potential organizational implications of LANs. Chapter 9 suggests that the implications of LANs, when implemented in organizations, may very well rest on two key organizational factors: (1) the organizational perception of the purpose of a LAN, and (2) the management style of the organization. Chapter 10 addresses the thorny issue of LAN implementation. Given the significant changes in organizational modes of communication made possible by LANs, implementation takes on great importance. This chapter proposes an implementation approach based on the ideals of socio-technical systems development and operationalized through participation.

In addition to the ten chapters, the book contains a glossary of terms and a number of appendices. The appendices provide detailed information on various specialized topics which are of a more limited interest to the general reader. This permits the main body of the text to concentrate on that subject matter of LANs which is of more general appeal, is less likely to change dramatically, and provides the core to understanding LANs.

Because of the tutorial nature of the text, individuals possessing a modest knowledge of computer technology and wanting to learn about LANs should find it within their range of comprehension. As such, the book should be of interest to advanced undergraduate and/or graduate students in computing or information systems, data processing professionals, individuals involved in planning and/or implementing office automation, and others who want to pick up an appreciation of local area networks.

We wish to acknowledge our many friends and colleagues who have helped us through their offering of suggestions, providing us with pertinent material on LANs, or by reviewing and commenting on portions of this text. We offer our thanks to Tony Cornford, Ian Galbraith, Frank Land, Chris Kennington, Ram Bannerjee, Bob Bird, and Ian Dallas. Particular thanks go to Sheik Yusuff whose painstaking efforts in the form of editorial assistance improved the readability of the text greatly.

Finally, we would like to thank Sue Coles and Leila Alberici for typing the original draft of this book.

London, England   VIV CHEONG
August 1982   RUDY HIRSCHHEIM

PART I:
CONCEPTS, CAPABILITIES,
and COMPARISONS

Introduction

Local area networks (LANs) have, with good reason, captured the imagination of many individuals over the past few years. With the growth of interest in the electronic office, local area networks are seen as the glue which would cement together the various information technology components of the automated office. LANs provide the facility through which microcomputers, word processors, workstations, and the like, communicate with one another and other office technologies such as data storage devices, facsimile devices, printers, intelligent copiers, computer output microfilm (COM), optical character readers, phototypesetters, voice and video handling devices, etc. This communication facility permits the implementation of electronic mail and the sharing of expensive resources.

Much of the interest in local area networks seems to have been sparked by the announcement made collectively by Digital, Intel, and Xerox (DIX) in May 1980 of a 'joint project to develop electrical, logical and protocol specifications for a local area communication network which the companies propose to use for many of their future products'. The basis of that announcement was, of course, Ethernet. Since then, numerous other LAN products have been announced: SILK—Hasler, WangNet—Wang, Data Ring—Toltec, Polynet—Logica, Xinet/Xibus—Xionics, Cambridge Ring—Acorn, TransRing 2000—SEEL, Planet—Racal Milgo, ODR-1—Syscon, Net/One—Ungermann-Bass, LocalNet—Sytek and NTL, BIS—Philips, and ARC—Datapoint. These systems all differ from one another in one or more dimensions. For example, some have a bus-based topology, while others are ring-based; most are baseband but a few are broadband; some use coaxial cable, others use twisted pairs; some are token passing systems, others use empty slots, while still others use contention transmission—normally CSMA-CD; SILK has a transmission speed in excess of 16 Mbps, while others have speeds of only 1–2 Mbps. The differences can be very great indeed, causing even more confusion than one might normally expect from a new technology.

But although local area networks can differ internally in a number of ways, they still share a number of common features. First, they are all restricted to a

1

relatively small geographic area—usually between several hundred metres and a few kilometres. LANs tend to be thought of in terms of one specific building or site. Secondly, LANs differ from wide area networks (WANs) or long haul networks in the size of bandwidths offered. LANs offer considerably greater bandwidths than WANs. (Bandwidths determine the data transmission rate of the communication facility and are based on the group of consecutive frequencies which constitute a band. A further treatment on the relationship between bandwidth and data rate can be found in Appendix D.) LANs use a technology which allows very high bandwidths to be implemented economically, thus permitting data rates in excess of 1 Mbps.[1] These high data rates are operationalized through a variety of media, viz., twisted pair cables, coaxial cables, and fibre optics. Thirdly, local area networks are designed to allow a large number of different devices to communicate with one another, and this would ultimately include products from a variety of manufacturers (this goal however is still some distance away). Additionally, with the peer-to-peer communication provided for by LANs, electronic mail is a much more economic proposition. Previously, electronic mail required the use of a host computer whereby messages had to be transmitted from the sender to a host computer, then from host to destination. This proved slow and costly. Lastly, LANs offer an impressively low bit error rate—1 in 10^{12} according to Cotton [11].

It must be noted that there are alternatives to the LAN approach for linking various devices together. For example, some office automation pundits are advocating the use of an intelligent switch which would handle all communication in an organization. It is, in essence, an enhanced private automatic branch exchange (PABX) and is based on extending the voice handling facilities on a telephone network to include data, text, and image communication. It is a centralized alternative to the distributed approach of the LAN. Unfortunately, since there is no such implemented product available, it is difficult to make meaningful comparisons between this approach and the LAN, except to state that such a system should not be susceptible to the failures that accompany 'traditional' centralized systems. Nevertheless, given the resources of AT&T and other telecommunications giants, this alternative may prove attractive. Additionally, the centralized nature of this approach may make it attractive to IBM, since it mirrors their philosophy towards data processing. And since IBM offers no LAN product at present, yet sells a PABX, this alternative may be the most natural. The one major question surrounding this approach is, will such a product be developed in a time frame which will make it competitive with LANs? The fear is that, by the time this product is available, there may be no market left; the market will have been saturated by LANs.

Another potential alternative is the micronetwork, e.g. Cluster/One, HiNet, Omninet, Z-Net, and Econet. They are smaller, slower, and more restrictive than a LAN, but could prove a cost-effective alternative if the desire is (ostensibly) only to link microcomputers and/or word processors together.

One of the other important issues yet to be resolved in the LAN field is that of standards. There are a number of bodies looking at standards issues but it seems unlikely that any one particular standard will be adopted universally. The lead organization in this area appears to be the IEEE with its Project 802. Project 802, after much deliberation, is considering two alternative strategies: one based on channel contention (CSMA-CD), the other on some form of token passing scheme. Other standards discussions have been undertaken by the US Department of Defense, the National Bureau of Standards, and the American National Standards Institute, but they are less well developed and fruitful, at the present time, than Project 802. Xerox, in the meantime, has been selling Ethernet licences to just about anyone who wants one at a nominal charge in an attempt to have a large number of vendors supplying Ethernet-compatible components. Wang and others have argued against an Ethernet standard as they feel any baseband standard is too limited. They want a standard which permits broadband systems to be developed. IBM has also been anti-Ethernet in an attempt to stop Ethernet becoming the official standard. Unfortunately, IBM has—at the moment—offered no real alternative, although it is known that they have been experimenting with some form of token passing ring system. For the potential LAN user, the standards debate promises to be an interesting—if not frustrating—issue which will continue to attract a great deal of attention.

In summary, LANs will probably be one of the key elements in the future automated office. As LAN technology develops, so will people's enthusiasm for LANs. Yet, much of the enthusiasm for LANs comes from what they purport to do rather than what the available products actually do. There is still more than just a little confusion surrounding local area networks. For example, what exactly is a local area network, i.e. how can it be defined; how do the various local area network approaches differ; how can local area networks be classified; what do some LAN products look like? These and many other questions continue to remain unanswered in many people's minds as the technology appears to have advanced more rapidly than our educational system's ability to keep abreast of these advancements. We hope to correct this imbalance by offering this two-part tutorial book on local area networks. Part I of this book addresses the thorny issue of defining a local area network by drawing together those characteristics cited most frequently by the various authors who have tried defining LANs in the past. LAN capabilities such as high data rates, low error rates, protocol simplicity, interconnection, etc., will also be discussed. Part I concludes by first offering a LAN classification scheme based on LAN topology and control strategies, and then comparing the two major LANs: the Cambridge Ring and Ethernet.

Part II looks at a number of practical issues related to LANs. These include a description of a number of LAN products, some factors which could be used in the evaluation of LANs, some future developments which could have a marked effect on LANs such as standards development and high-level protocols, and finally some important considerations to be made when implementing LANs in organizations.

Chapter 1
Defining a LAN

There are many LAN definitions proffered by various authors, but none which is generally accepted. Dictionary definitions of 'local' and 'network' make no useful contribution towards clarification either. The vexing issue of a LAN definition will continue unabated unless the parameters of the subject can be more closely confined, an aspect that has not escaped the recognition of Freeman and Thurber [1]. These authors have identified many characteristics upon which LAN definitions have been founded. Such characteristics include speed, distance, transmission medium, switching technology, percentage of traffic not passing through a gateway, single organization proprietorship, single function usage, use of distributed processing, network configuration and/or the relationship to I/O channels. This chapter looks at a number of these characteristics and how they are used by the various authors attempting to define LANs.

Thurber and Freeman [2], who have spent a great deal of time assimilating various LAN definitions, recognize the great difficulty in developing one which would be universally accepted. They note that in the short history of local networks only 'one real attempt has been made to develop a definition of [local area networks]' and that attempt was theirs. Basically, Thurber and Freeman assert that, in order for a LAN to be defined as a class of network-like systems, three basic properties should be satisfied. They are:

(1) single organization proprietorship;
(2) distances involved are of the order of a few miles and in the general locality;
(3) the deployment of some type of switching technology.

Single organization proprietorship means that in general only one organization owns the network. Whether more than one organization can use the network is not apparent, although it does not appear to be precluded. Distances involved of the order of a few miles is meant to distinguish LANs from wide area networks which cover great distances. This appears necessary as LANs often use the same technology, i.e. packet switching, as WANs. The deployment of some type of switching technology refers to the fact that LANs employ a technology which allows connection of the appropriate stations when messages are to be transmitted and received. (It is noteworthy that based on Thurber and Freeman's definition, PABXs are not necessarily differentiated from LANs.)

The above postulates are imprecise, but are not markedly dissimilar to a definition advanced by Tanenbaum [3]. Tanenbaum defines LANs in terms of 'single ownership by a single organisation, a diameter of not more than a few kilometres, and a total data rate exceeding 1 Mbps'. Here the commonalities with Thurber and Freeman lie in 'single ownership by a single organisation' and 'a diameter of not more than a few kilometres'.[2] The difference in Tanenbaum's definition is that of a total data rate exceeding 1 Mbps as contrasted to 'the deployment of some type of switching technology'.

Another definition of LANs is offered in the Seybold report [4]. Here LANs are defined somewhat loosely:

> A local area network is one that interconnects devices using non public signal conductors within an area of 5-10 miles, often considerably less.

The property of 'single organizational ownership' is conspicuous by its absence in the Seybold definition but the geographical locality has now been quantified as 5-10 miles as opposed to 'a few miles' [2] or 'a few kilometres' [3].

Farber and Larson [5] propose a definition of LANs which indicates the difficulty inherent in LAN definition. They define a LAN as 'typically a packet network, limited in geographical scope'. Note how this definition is very general and may not adequately distinguish LANs from other networks.

Thus far, the four LAN definitions examined have attempted to define LANs from a consideration of the properties possessed by LANs. An alternative approach would be a definition that considers the position that LANs occupy in relation to other arrangements of data communication hardware.

Metcalfe and Boggs regard LANs as filling a 'logical gap' in a gamut which has remote networking and multiprocessing at the extremes [6]:

> Near the middle of this spectrum is local area networking, the interconnection of computers, to gain the resource sharing of computer networking and the parallelism of multiprocessing.

Table 1 shows how Metcalfe and Boggs view LANs as filling this 'logical gap'.

Note that the bit rate offered by Metcalfe and Boggs, which ranges from 0.1 to 10 Mbps, differs from Tanenbaum's definition which states that the bit rate exceeds 1 Mbps [3].[3]

Metcalfe and Boggs' treatment of 'separation' (or distance) as an important aspect in discussing LANs is shared by Clark *et al.* [7] who regard LANs as occupying an intermediate position, as detailed in Table 2.

TABLE 1

Activity	Separation (km)	Bit rate (Mbps)
Remote networks	<10	<0.1
LANs	10–0.1	0.1–10
Multiprocessors	<0.1	>10

TABLE 2

Category	Distance (km)
Long haul networks	$10^{-2}-10^{4}$
LANs	$10^{-2}-10^{1}$
Computer system I/O buses	$10^{-4}-10^{-1}$

Clark *et al.* develop their definition of LANs by starting with Farber and Larson's [5] definition, 'typically a packet communication network, limited in geographical scope', and including three hardware elements (a transmission medium, a transmission control mechanism, and a network interface) plus a set of software protocols (implemented in the host computers or other network devices which control the transmission of information). In the opinion of Clark and his co-authors, it is this combined hardware-software approach to communication that distinguishes networks from other arrangements of data communication hardware, and is therefore necessary in the defining of LANs.

A number of authors have attempted to emphasize the communication aspect of LANs within the context of an organization; see for example Wilkes [8] who discusses LANs in terms of:

... a communication system for interconnecting computers within its own building, or its own site (which is what I take local area to signify)...

Similarly, the National Bureau of Standards [9] state:

A major distinction between local and global networks is the higher degree of control that a single organization is likely to have over the design and operation of a local network.

These two definitions suggest that there is some explicit (and implicit) effort being made to acknowledge the need to consider user-oriented criteria as well as technologically oriented criteria when defining LANs. The recognition that organizations will probably play some part in the design and operation of a LAN is a major step forward. Yet, not everyone would agree that this recognition means very much. McQuillan, for example, maintains that the design of networks has proceeded in reverse, viz. networks are designed before the full acknowledgement of user requirements [10].

Note the LAN definitions offered have a strong bias towards the computing/data environment. It might even be argued that these definitions differ little—if any—from those of local computer networks (LCN). (A LCN could be regarded as differing from a LAN in that the former is solely concerned with data communications, whereas the latter attempts to satisfy other local communication requirements.) Indeed, this is correct, and reflects the heavy computing bias that there is in the LAN area. To put it differently, most LAN definitions have come from the data communications literature. This is so because LANs are seen as an evolutionary development by the data communications community. This is a position which may be disputed by some who see LANs much more in the context of voice and/or video communication and which perhaps manifests itself in discussions on whether LANs should be baseband or broadband.

This chapter has presented a number of definitions of LANs offered by various authors, but it is clear that none would be universally accepted. A number of specific properties, when taken collectively, do seem to capture the spirit of what a LAN is but, when looked at individually, each property is somewhat problematic. For example, single organization proprietorship would appear to be a criterion accepted by most but this may not be the case for too much longer.[4] Additionally, single organization proprietorship seems to imply that only one organization would use a specific LAN. Yet one can think of a number of circumstances where a number of different organizations might want access to a specific LAN, e.g. in an office complex. The criterion of close geographical distance, again, would be acceptable to most—if not all—but the problem arises when one attempts to quantify 'close'. As was seen in this chapter, 'close' was variously defined as 'a few miles' [2], 'a few kilometres' [3], '5-10 miles' [4], '0.1-10 km' [6], '0.01-10 km' [7], and 'covering distances measured in 100's of metres to distances measured in kilometres' [11]. It is clear that the authors discussing distance did so in an attempt to distinguish LANs from WANs. WANs, it must be remembered, tend to cover very large geographical areas (tens of kilometres to thousands of kilometres). Similarly, LANs differ from WANs in their data rates; LANs have much greater data rates. Thus it is not surprising that many authors used data rate as a criterion in their definitions of LANs. Metcalfe and Bogg's [6] range of 0.1-10 Mbps does seem to be acceptable to most, but it is clear that not all would agree with this range (see for example [4]). Additional issues such as the degree of control that an organization could (should) exert over the design and operation of a LAN, and to what extent a LAN is conceived as a technology which interconnects more than just computer/data devices, are much more perplexing issues upon which agreement may never be reached.

In conclusion, no attempt has been made here to develop an all-embracing LAN definition, but it is hoped that the reader has been given some insight into the intricacies involved. It should be clear that the real issue of defining a LAN will remain 'thorny' as long as the assumptions regarding LANs themselves remain undefined.

Chapter 2
Causal Factors in LAN Development

There are a number of economic and technological factors that have no doubt led to the development of LANs. In particular, two factors have perhaps contributed the most to LAN development: (1) the decline in PTT cost/performance and the continued technological progress; and (2) the evolution of office automation and the trend towards distributed systems.

2.1 The Decline in PTT Cost/Performance and the Concomitant Technological Progress

There is a close relationship between LANs and WANs, as their structure and protocols are rooted in packet communication, whilst their hardware is derived from both network and computer hardware technology. Accompanying the widespread understanding and acceptance of the former has been the dramatic decrease in the cost of hardware. These factors have allowed the increasing demand for high data rates and low-cost communication amongst the vast variety of machines to be satisfied [7].

However, if the primary objective of the network is the facilitation of communication between devices, is the local need not already met by the teleprocessing front ends of mainframes and the relevant services provided by the PTTs? 'No' must clearly be the response, as a terminal population closely grouped in one fairly tight geographical location is considerably different from the far wider physical dispersion of the terminals of an entire teleprocessing system. The latter have had to rely upon the provision of PTT services (usually for legal reasons) where the cost of long haul transmission has been the all-pervading consideration, although the situation is slowly changing [8].

Under such constraints, bandwidth has been a precious commodity. Much effort has been directed towards its conservation, e.g. multiplexing, resource sharing, code compression techniques, etc., whilst simultaneously attempting to overcome the disadvantages of working with an analogue network and its susceptibility to errors when transmitting digital signals. Such errors have necessitated devices such as modems and error detection techniques.

The large physical distributions involved result in the inevitable requirement for techniques to reduce transmission cost, e.g. polling regimes, route optimization algorithms, and the general need to resort to public switched networks where the amount of traffic does not justify a dedicated circuit. Restricting the geographical area enables the utilization of wideband circuits, alleviating LANs from the traditional WAN constraints [7]. Consequently, as bandwidth is no longer a limited resource, LANs are relieved of all routing and switching problems and can offer a completely different range of services through their different mode of operation, which is afforded by their limited geographical scope. This renders the proprietary network strategies, e.g. SNA, IPA, and Decnet, and the telecommunications network offerings, e.g. X.21, X.25, of limited relevance [3, 12].

Although the realization of high bandwidth connections between all participating parties is possible, networking technology is primarily concerned with its cost-effectiveness by sharing communication facilities. In this respect, the declining cost of digital circuit elements has been a significant development, facilitating the construction of useful and sophisticated LANs. These LANs can provide a dynamically allocatable bandwidth to meet bursty user/system communication demands, high bandwidth (1 Mbps), very high accuracy (one undetected error bit in 10^{12}), high network availability/reliability, and utilizing low-cost hardware whose price continues to decline. These facts have generated the interest in LANs [11, 12].

2.2 The Evolution of Office Automation and the Trend Towards Distributed Systems

As stated at the beginning of this section, the decline in the cost performance of the PTTs and technological advancement, in particular the microprocessor, have not been solely responsible for the generation of interest in LANs. It is not intended to undervalue the ramifications of microprocessor development, but there are other reasons for this interest. These are the growth of office automation and the trend towards distributed processing.[5]

Within the office context itself, LANs will undoubtedly occupy an influential role in the architecture of office systems [7]. Consider the following facts. Less than 25% of all written and verbal communications involve direct interaction with people outside a company. Furthermore, 90% of all information is distributed within half a mile and in excess of 75% is distributed within 600 ft [4]. The explanation is not difficult to comprehend. Most institutions are organized departmentally and physically located to facilitate access to the same information files. This also allows conferring during the normal course of work. Thus, the importance of the role played by LANs in facilitating resource sharing, whether it is the sharing of information files and storage capacity or the sharing of printing resources and remote communications services, is not difficult to appreciate.

The implication is that as a significant proportion of attention has been and will continue to be focused on seeking compatible technological solutions for intra-company communications, LANs will grow in importance.[6] But the analysis of organizational information distribution is not the only reason for interest in LANs.

The application of various forms of new information technology for the improvement of communications and the elimination of unproductive paper handling operations in the office, e.g. electronic mail and text editing, has created a demand for high-speed, flexible, and reliable office communication systems [14]. The increasing complexity of organizational and business functions has also meant that the management of information has become an integral part of the modern office.[7] Distributed office information systems can facilitate the evolution towards the automated office by reducing the initial investment required and permitting growth in accordance with organizational needs and structure [15].

Tanenbaum attributes the interest in LANs to the requirement to interconnect computers and the desire to benefit from functionally distributed systems [3]. A practical example of the interest in LANs has been summarized by Spratt from the University of Kent [16]. These reasons include:

(1) the allowance of an evolving situation as regards the installation (and removal) of computing equipment;
(2) stand-alone communications;
(3) a linked mainframe permitting a remote job entry facility connected to more powerful systems at regional computer centres;
(4) the sharing of peripherals;
(5) centralized filing.

Alternatively, Thurber and Freeman actually apportion this interest to two diverse groups [1]. The first comprises those individuals reaching the boundaries of their current systems and who regard the development of LANs as a method of extension and improvement. The second group seeks the incorporation and utilization of new concepts such as distributed processing. These authors give no indication as to whether it is possible to be a member of both groups.

Finally, to exemplify the need for LANs, the following is Dallas' observation of the computer laboratory at the University of Kent [17]:

> The situation which existed at Kent was no doubt symptomatic of that in other campuses, with a rats' nest of cables, both within the Computer Laboratory, and campus-wide. Whenever two pieces of equipment needed to be connected together, then this required a new cable. As more and more terminals, departmental minis and micros were being installed, the situation was going to become steadily worse. The sensible way forward appeared to be the introduction of the local area network.

Wilkes and Wheeler offer a simple suggestion regarding why LANs have arrived, viz. because there was a need [18]:

> There is a need for a system that would allow interconnection of computers and devices within a building and be capable of operating at a data rate substantially in advance of that provided by conventional communication techniques.

Chapter 3

The Capabilities and Desirable Features of LANs

If LANs are to fulfil a need, they must possess some potential that would enable them to satisfy a set of requirements. This section will thus examine the capabilities and desirable features of LANs and the extent to which the claims for LANs are justified.

First, what must any standard networking system offer? Clearly, one aspect would be that such a system must permit growth in size and type of office services. It must also allow the interconnection with systems and services from other vendors through devices such as protocol translation gateways. Furthermore, such systems must display robustness and reliability. They must facilitate installation, servicing, and expansion without the disruption of existing network users [15].

The intended use of LANs to serve a local user population means that they must meet a different set of requirements from WANs. These local users could be composed of unbuffered asynchronous terminals, buffered synchronous terminals, and computers which may operate in either mode.

It is possible to categorize the attributes of LANs as those which are technical and those which are non-technical in nature. This chapter is thus divided accordingly.

3.1 Technical Characteristics

3.1.1 Data rate

The requirement for a high *data rate* that LANs should be able to satisfy has two primary aspects. First, LANs should be able to support the maximum data rate between any pair of communicating stations. Secondly, any communication between two terminals operating at different speeds requires LAN support in terms of flow control and storage [11].

The *high bandwidth* and *low delay attributes* of LANs allow the distribution of multiprocessors. These may utilize the type of information sharing commonly associated with multiprocessor systems sharing primary memory.

11

In addition, exploitation of the high bandwidth allows protocol simplification and, consequently, the minimization of control or overhead information is no longer of major concern. This can be extended to other aspects of LAN protocols, e.g. allocation schemes of network bandwidth, flow control, and error detection and correction.

3.1.2 Connectivity

The *connectivity* requirements of LANs are determined by the expected traffic patterns among the stations to be served and the reliability of the service. The employment of dedicated point-to-point connections may only be feasible when a few stations are involved, but there may be a requirement for a switching service if the need to place calls alternatively to other stations exists. This may then be provided in situations which demand alternative routing to ensure the availability and survivability of the service.

3.1.3 Low error rates

The availability and variety of error detection techniques which allow LANs to attain *low error rates* fall into two general categories: first, those techniques that utilize send and receive terminals only; and secondly, those that utilize intelligent devices within the network itself. The techniques also vary in complexity, from simple character parity checks to complex cyclic redundancy checksums (CRCs). The latter permits the achievement of an arbitrarily low undetected error rate at the expense of extending the length of the CRC. In practice, the undetected error rate is reported to be 1 in 10^{12} [11].

3.1.4 Geographical dispersion

The *geographical dispersion* of LANs is often described in a rather vague fashion, e.g. limited geographical area, yet the variance in geographical dispersion could affect the suitability of various LAN technologies.

Consider, for example, the categories and distances presented in Table 3.

LANs are normally intended to meet the requirements of the same building

TABLE 3

Category	Distance
Same component	0–1 m
Same system	1–10 m
Same room	10s m
Same building	100s m
Same campus	1–10 km
Same city	10s km
Same region	100s km

or the same campus [14].[8] However, the contextual requirements may be sufficiently different to indicate the superiority of one LAN over another under one set of conditions [11].

3.1.5 Network services

The provision of additional network services can be achieved by the integration of intelligent devices in such a manner that sending and receiving terminals are decoupled from each other. Such services include speed and code conversion, echoing support for device-specific characteristics such as carriage return delays and line widths. The LAN then should provide storage and processing, either in the subscriber interface or in some intelligent device within the network itself.

Speed conversion enables terminals which operate at different data rates to communicate with each other. Two speed translations are usually needed as the network itself operates at a data rate which differs from the sending and receiving terminals—one for connecting the sending terminal to the network, the other for connecting the network to the receiving terminal. The handling of these speed mismatches is achieved by intermediate buffering, in combination with flow control mechanisms.

Code conversion is also necessary for communication as terminals use different internal codes. The translation of messages into a standard format and the subsequent retranslation to the specific requirements of the receiving terminals is all done by the network. Alternatively, code conversion may be achieved by permitting the specification of requirements at call placement time and the occurrence of direct translation of codes from sender and receiver terminals, often by intelligent devices resident in the terminal interface.

Echoing support may reduce the transmission load on the communication links of the network. This support eliminates the echo from the destination terminal for full duplex operation. Instead, an echo is provided by a device in the network closer to the sending terminal interface or by an intelligent device in the network closer to the secondary terminal. This service could significantly alleviate the network of its transmission load for full duplex asynchronous terminals.

Various alternatives for *data forwarding conditions* exist which allow the network to assemble and transmit packets on the basis of the accumulation of some number of input characters, the passage of some time interval or the receipt of some particular character (e.g. end of line, calling for retransmission). If and when data are blocked in buffers prior to transmission, it is possible for the network to provide local editing of the input text to ensure the correctness of data before forwarding.

The *device-specific support* potential of LANs allows for the accommodation of different terminal characters, such as carriage return delay requirements, which needs the insertion of extra padding characters, line length and screen size, and operator-controlled paging.

3.1.6 Interconnection with other networks

The ability to *interconnect with other networks*[9] is likely to be an important attribute that LANs should possess. This may be motivated by economic reasons or simply by the needs of the users. Such needs may take the following form:

    (i) a computerized mail system in which messages to and from LAN users can be exchanged via a WAN (LAN-WAN);[10]

    (ii) access to specialized computing resources required on an occasional basis but which is economically unjustified on a local basis;

    (iii) communication between LANs (LAN-LAN).

To conclude this half of the chapter, it is interesting to note that the characteristics outlined here feature prominently in the four goals set out by the MIT Laboratory of Computer Science for the establishment of a LAN [19]. These four goals were:

    (i) the interconnection of desk-top computers and typically large computers (connectivity);

    (ii) the application of clusters of two or more computers to specific tasks (device-specific support);

    (iii) the extension to a campus or site-wide network (interconnection with other networks);

    (iv) a bandwidth in the 1–10 Mbps range, so that file transfer can be a convenient part of interactive operations (data rate).

Saltzer and Pogran [19] recognized, however, that the choice of technology was only one consideration. There were other more 'mundane' issues which also had to be considered. These mundane issues were not technologically oriented and are the subject of the second half of this chapter.

3.2 Non-Technical Characteristics

Although the technical capabilities of LANs are important, there are other important requirements of LANs which are not technical in nature. It is arguable that these non-technical characteristics are of, at least, equal importance.

Saltzer and Pogran [19], for example, claim that the four desirable features described in the previous half of this section only tell part of the story:

> This set of goals led us to conclude that the best technology choice has little to do with usual analyses of performance, collision rate or bit error rates, but rather more mundane issues such as which technology is easiest to install, reconfigure and maintain in a typical office building.

3.2.1 Capacity

Similarly, Joyce maintains that designers should seek to combine three objectives: capacity, reliability, and flexibility [14]. LANs must possess sufficient communication capacity for document transfer without extensive delay and without the need for coordination between different network users, if electronic document transmission is eventually to substitute paper handling in the office.

3.2.2 Reliability

Reliability is also of paramount importance. If the productivity gains available through office automation are to be achieved, new automated systems will have to be dependable, otherwise users may well continue to use their old systems.

3.2.3 Flexibility

Flexibility in the type of equipment to be connected to the LAN is also important. The usefulness of a network is significantly reduced if its design must be tailored to specific types of equipment and their physical locations.

3.2.4 Vendor support

Additionally the issue of vendor independence must also be considered. Essentially, it is preferable to have the greater flexibility of a number of vendors working to an agreed specification than single vendors working to their own particular standard [20]. (This will be discussed in greater detail in Part II.)

If a LAN is formally specified and made publicly available, it is possible that other vendors will implement the particular specification rather than develop their own. Their motivation would be the hope that they could sell their equipment to users who have already installed the network, but there is little doubt that a widely accepted network standard would be a significant advantage to many companies, users and vendors alike [4][11]. (This is something which Xerox has attempted with Ethernet.)

Therefore, any potential implementation of a LAN must be apprized of the relevance of the product and the technology and the maintenance offered by the vendor. Indirect costs, such as disruption through implementation and installation, staff and user training, support and documentation, are just some of the other factors that also require appraisal. It is reasonably apparent, at least for the present, that LANs are not an off-the-shelf, plug-in, panacea for all local area computer communication needs. The marketing of LANs by their vendors has caused some concern as is expressed below:

> Xerox has been to blame for spreading the idea that local networks will be the answer to all the interconnection problems of the electronic office. Just because different devices work to the same communications protocol, it

doesn't mean that black boxes won't be needed. For example, each word processor has a different method for underlining.

Dale Kutwick, Yankee Group, Boston [21]

My advice to potential users of local networks would be, don't commit yourselves. There is no one yet who can offer all the facilities you will need.

Christopher Ellis, Nexos Office Equipment [21]

3.2.5 Other considerations

Other factors that may be cited may be drawn from the experiences of the University of Kent [17]. Apart from considerations such as whether the LAN could be purchased 'off the shelf', its cost, and its ease of implementation, the University of Kent recognized that other management issues had to be tackled. These included control and accounting procedures, fault finding and fixing procedures, maintenance testing, commissioning and repair of equipment, and the need for a coherent policy for extending the capabilities of the LAN supported by adequate documentation to assist users via 'friendly' interfaces [20,171].

Chapter 4

Classifying LANs

At present, there is a very diverse range of LANs available. Some exist as LAN products being offered by various vendors and others exist as specially constructed 'one off' implementations, usually in the computer laboratories of research institutions whose interests in LANs are predominantly of an experimental and innovative nature. With such a multitude of LANs some classification ought to be possible. This chapter, therefore, discusses the various classification schemes offered and presents a synthesis (Table 5) of these schemes.

Wood has categorized LANs in terms of the degree of sophistication that the particular network displays and in terms of the way the nodes may be interconnected [23]. This crude method of classification is based on the assertion that there are as many gradients of networks as there are computers and it is important that their different capabilities be appreciated prior to any comparison.

Here, the least sophisticated class of LANs are those which only permit the connection to the same family of vendor equipment. These would include micronetworks which would operate at relatively slow speeds and distances, e.g. Cluster/One for Apple II from Nestar/Zynar; Omninet for Apple II from Corvus; Z-Net for MCZ-2 from Zilog.

At a higher level of sophistication, there exist the LANs which address the 'incompatibles' market. Here the objective is to provide a means of exchanging data in an environment which has grown up with a variety of mainframes, micros, word processors, and other technical devices. Examples of this category are Ethernet from Xerox, DEC, Intel; Net/One from Ungermann-Bass; Polynet from Logica; and Data Ring from Toltec.

In the highest level of sophistication, there are those systems which are capable of providing: (a) the local processing capability of a personal computer network; (b) intercomputer communication of a universal network; (c) powerful data management capabilities; and (d) the high speeds and sophisticated software essential for handling voice and document image in addition to data communication. Examples of this cateogry are Xinet/Xibus from Xionics, LocalNet from NTL, and SILK from Hasler.

TABLE 4

LANs	Transmission rate (bps)
Group 1	2 400– 19 200
Group 2	19 200– 1 000 000
Group 3	1 000 000– 10 000 000
Group 4	10 000 000–300 000 000

In a similar vein, the Seybold Report [4] recognizes four groups of LANs, categorized in terms of bit rate (Table 4). The groups are described as follows:

Group 1 is intended to interconnect many small or personal computers and, since the main consideration is low cost, network bandwidth is sacrificed.

Group 2 emphasizes bandwidth to a greater extent, but costs are moderated. This group of LANs is constructed with readily available microprocessor and interface chips.

Group 3 provides significantly greater bandwidth at the expense of more costly interfaces.

Group 4 provides very great bandwidth with the associated higher cost interfaces.

These classification schemes—based on level of sophistication or bit rate—are, however, of limited value. For example, there is no reason why a network which only allows the same family of equipment to be attached to it should be considered unsophisticated.[12] In fact, many LANs which fit into this category are really quite technically sophisticated. Thus, it is suggested that a more appropriate way to classify LANs is by their topologies and/or control strategies. Most of the LAN classification schemes appearing in the literature are of this variety.

Table 5 attempts to assimilate some of the various taxonomies offered in the literature. It is hoped that through this synthesis a better appreciation of the various classes of LANs may be gained. A few comments regarding Table 5 should be made at this point.

(1) The LAN topologies have been written in capital letters to distinguish them from the control strategies.

(2) The various LAN classes that have been recognized by the authors considered here have been italicized, e.g. *STAR*, *BUS*, *contention*.

(3) If the authors have used the topology as a means of classifying LANs and then within each topological class the control strategies associated with the topology are used as a means of subclassification, this has been denoted in the column heading by (i) TOPOLOGY, (ii) control, e.g. Clark *et al.* [7], Seybold Report [4], Joyce [14], Weitzman [25]. Yet as will become apparent from the next sections of this chapter, a number of network control strategies are suited to particular topologies.[13]

(4) However, if the authors have in general used only one attribute as a means of classification, that attribute is expressed in the column heading, e.g. control in Cotton [11] and Tanenbaum [3]. In both these cases *RING* appears and this obviously refers to topology. Thus, the authors concerned have not solely used control strategies as a means of classification and it would

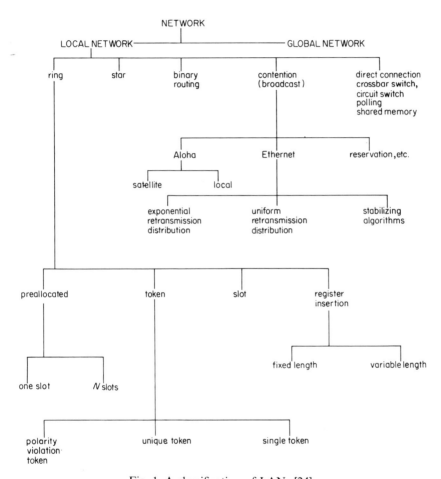

Fig. 1. A classification of LANs [24].

complicate this taxonomic comparison if this were also expressed in the column headings. In the opinion of the authors, Cotton [11] and Tanenbaum [3] have implicitly emphasized the control aspects of LANs rather than their topologies.

(5) Consider the classification of Hopper [24] (see Fig. 1) where there seemed to be no emphasis on either the topology or the control aspects of

LANs. Hence the column heading has been expressed as TOPOLOGY/control.

(6) The classification drawn up by Weitzman [25] does not include any centralized systems which possess star or hierarchical topologies, because of the consideration of distributed microcomputer and minicomputer systems only. However, centralized control strategies are considered in the category of *SHARED BUS*, but appear in Table 5 under *shared memory*. Thus, this representation of Weitzman's classification is not in the strictest sense totally accurate, as the subcategories of 'centrally controlled, polled bus', 'interrupt driven, centrally controlled bus' and 'centrally controlled, slotted bus', which appear under *shared memory*, should appear under *SHARED BUS*. However, there is some justification for this in terms of placing these subcategories in this position along the continuum of centralized to decentralized. Weitzman specifically includes time-shared/common bus as a subcategory of *shared memory*, but makes no real mention of control strategies which allow the bus to be time-shared. As Tanenbaum [3] points out, centralized control strategies can be used on shared memory systems which are connected to a common bus and such strategies could include those of the 'centrally controlled, polled bus', the 'interrupt driven, centrally controlled bus', and the 'centrally controlled, slotted bus'. Such systems are thus essentially distributed in topology, but are centrally controlled and hence have been included in Table 5 in the middle of the centralized/decentralized continuum. This illustrates that decentralization and centralization are multifaceted terms.

(7) Table 5 shows that these classes of LANs may be accommodated in a continuum with centralized approaches at one end and completely decentralized approaches at the other.

(8) This taxonomy which places classes of LANs along a continuum of centralized to decentralized approaches or strategies does appear to be a useful way to categorize them, as it takes into account most of the important criteria written about in the literature. For example, LAN topologies and control strategies fit in reasonably well in the taxonomy. Yet not all would agree that such a continuum exists; or even if it did, that LAN classification might be somewhat arbitrary. Actually, as can be seen from Table 5, this discussion is somewhat academic. Most existing LAN architectures, viz. rings and contention buses, are placed on the 'decentralized' side of the continuum. Given that LANs are viewed as a distributed technology by most, this categorization should pose little problem. Some disagreement is possible, however, on the taxonomy's categorization of strategies such as local non-switched, local circuit switched, local message switched, etc., as more 'centralized' strategies. Although these strategies may not inherently be either centralized or decentralized in their own right, their use has historically been in centralized systems. Thus, they have been placed on the 'centralized' side of the continuum. Given that few, if any, LANs employ such strategies, little debate would seem warranted. A further elaboration on the various aspects of the centralized/decentralized continuum follows.

TABLE 5   A comparison of some authors' taxonomies.

Degree of distribution	Author: Attributes: (i) TOPOLOGY (ii) control	Clark [7] (i) TOPOLOGY (ii) control	Cotton [11] control	Hopper [24] (i) TOPOLOGY (ii) control	Tanenbaum [3] control	Seybold Report [4] (i) TOPOLOGY (ii) control	Joyce [14] (i) TOPOLOGY (ii) control	Weitzman [25] (i) TOPOLOGY (ii) control
centralized		*STAR*	*local circuit switch* local message switch local packet switch local non-switched hierarchical	*STAR* circuit switch		*STAR*	*STAR* circuit switch message switch	
tightly coupled				*shared memory* polling	*shared memory* central arbiter	*TREE* polling		*shared memory* time-shared/common bus centrally controlled polled bus interrupt driven, centrally controlled bus
					dedicated single daisy chaining			
				crossbar switch	crosspoint switch multiported memory			centrally controlled, slotted bus crossbar switch multibus/multiport
decentralized			fully connected					*LOOP* control token fixed-size slots delay insertion
		RING daisy chain control token register insertion contention	*RING* 'caboose' control slot register insertion	*RING* preallocated token slot register insertion	*RING* token slotted register insertion contention	*RING* token passing slotting	*RING* *LOOP* token passing	
		BUS contention	*contention* carrier sense unrestrained CSMA–CD	*contention* Aloha Ethernet	*carrier sense* 1–CSMA Ethernet collision free	*SNAKE* carrier sense CSMA–CD	*BUS* contention	*SHARED BUS* Global Multiple Access Bus Global TDM Bus Global FDM Bus

4.1 Centralized Control Strategies

These are strategies or approaches which are felt to be of a more centralized nature. As was discussed above, these strategies are not necessarily *inherently* centralized, but have, nevertheless, historically been associated with centralized systems. It must be added that these approaches have been in relatively widespread use in comparison to their decentralized counterparts, e.g. rings. Additionally, they may be viewed as being the older and more established approaches. As such, they were more widely used in the early days of data communication and networks where a central computer (usually a mainframe) had control of the network.

4.1.1 Local non-switched networks (LNSNs)

These represent the most basic approach upon which LANs may be based. This involves the interconnection of all the devices that need to communicate by means of dedicated point-to-point links. Different transmission media and interfaces may be utilized according to the nature of the devices communicating over the link and this situation may be quite satisfactory for a LAN with limited requirements, but such an approach does not facilitate flexibility and adaptability.

There are two subcategories of LNSNs: (a) fully connected and (b) hierarchical networks.

A LNSN may be *fully connected*, which means that each node needing to communicate with another may do so because each node in the network is connected to each other via a dedicated channel. Fully connected nodes (Fig. 2a) possess as many channels as there are other nodes and communication is not possible unless a dedicated channel is supplied. If there are N devices, the number of channels is $N(N-1)/2$. The nature of each channel is permanent (e.g. by a hardwired circuit or leased line) and hence the channel's capacity is wasted when stations are not communicating. Thus, completely connected LAN topologies offer the lowest delay but are expensive [24]. No speed or code conversion or flow control is provided as the devices must communicate at a common speed and code over the link which tightly couples the two stations.

Hierarchical networks (Fig. 2b) represent another basic approach to constructing simple LANs. This is characterized by the presence of intermediate nodes between the two communicating parties, which may operate in a store-and-forward mode. Ordinarily, no switching is performed since there will be only a single path between two communicating nodes.

4.1.2 Local circuit switched networks (LCSNs)

This is another basic approach but offers more flexibility than LNSNs. LCSNs possess configurations which allow a node to communicate with a

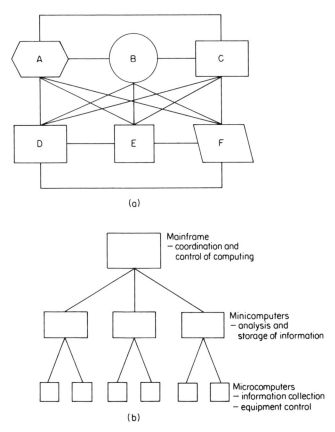

Fig. 2. (a) Completely connected and (b) hierarchical
topologies.

variety of other nodes and thus are similar, in configuration, to that of a star
(Fig. 3a). A channel can be established between two stations whenever they
need to communicate and there is no switching delay in conveying the data,
once the channel has been set up. Thus, each connection appears as a
dedicated point-to-point link. Existing LCSNs, such as the public telephone
network, have little provision for terminal support services such as speed and
code conversion, nor can the network exercise anything but the simplest form
of flow control.

LCSNs sometimes utilize *multidrop lines* (Fig. 3b) which are used when
there is a central controller employing polling. Multidrop lines facilitate the
operation of a network when any one of a variety of polling strategies is
applied. The two most common are *roll call polling*, in which the central
controller invites each station to transmit in some predetermined order, and
hub go-ahead polling, where each station that has nothing to transmit passes
the poll along to the next station in turn.

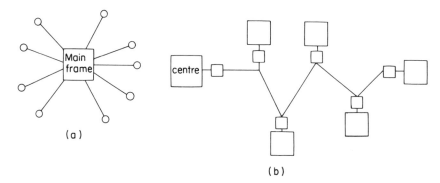

Fig. 3. (a) Star and (b) multidropped configurations.

4.1.3 Local message and packet switched networks (LMSNs and LPSNs)

These types of networks are based on a message/packet switching approach. A message switching processor functions by receiving data, storing it in memory while the intended route is determined, and then retransmitting the data on the correct output line. Code or protocol conversion may also be provided by the central processor and speed conversion is intrinsic, since the input and output lines operate independently at the appropriate speed for the terminal or particular line. A network of switching computers can be made to operate as a message or packet switching system with alternate routing, but for local requirements a single switch may be all that is needed. Transmission from high- speed to low-speed devices means that flow control must be exercised when buffers in the switch become overloaded. Local high-speed devices can be interfaced through high-speed channels (provided such interfaces exist on the computer selected as the network switch). And as the switch serves to decouple sending and receiving terminals, all network services may be provided for.

It is clear that the star configuration is particularly suited to LCSNs, LMSNs, and LPSNs and thus, at this juncture, a few observations will be made concerning this topology.

The need for each node to make routing decisions is eliminated by localizing all message routing in one central node. This simple topology is suited where the normal pattern of communications in the network conforms to its physical dispersion, i.e. where a number of secondary nodes communicate with one primary node such as in a time-sharing system.

If the normal pattern of communication is not between one primary node and several secondary nodes, but is more general (communication among all nodes), then the reliability aspect detracts from the star configuration. The whole operation of the network is entirely reliant on the correct functioning of the central node, which may be a fairly large machine as it must have sufficient capacity to perform all routing functions and handle simultaneous conversations. For these reasons, the cost and difficulty of making the central node sufficiently dependable may more than offset any benefit derived from the simplicity of the other nodes [4,7,14].

4.1.4 Shared memory systems

Shared memory systems can be regarded as being situated nearer to centralized control strategies on the continuum of centralized to decentralized strategies (see Table 5). To some degree, some of the control strategies employed by shared memory systems are not dissimilar to those employed on other more distributed systems, but can be regarded as lying closer to the centralized extreme of the continuum in the respect that this class of system is more 'tightly coupled' than the more 'loosely coupled' ring and contention networks. These latter two classes of system (discussed later in the chapter) do not involve the use of control strategies which determine how a population of processors cooperate in sharing a common memory and hence are referred to as 'loosely coupled' and not 'tightly coupled' systems.

The terms 'tightly coupled' and 'loosely coupled' deserve a little more explanation. The former refers to the ability of all processors in the system to access each other's memory. However, memory is not the only resource that is shared. Sharing also applies to I/O devices and other peripherals.

'Loosely coupled' systems do not employ this concept of memory sharing. Instead, each processor possesses its own separate and independent memory space. This permits concurrent processes to be executed in an asynchronous manner in each of the processors, whereas 'tightly coupled' systems require some means of synchronization for the processors to access the common memory. In this sense, 'tightly coupled' systems may be regarded as less decentralized than more 'loosely coupled' systems, but as will be observed, some of the control strategies employed render this statement somewhat problematic, as decentralized control strategies may be used.

In general, LANs are more 'tightly coupled' than WANs and the most extreme form of this occurs when a collection of processors share a common address space or use the same memory. This is sometimes referred to as a multiprocessor architecture. In this respect, Tanenbaum [3], Hopper [24], and Weitzman [25] regard shared memory systems as an alternative class of communication architecture where these systems are composed of a number of processors separated by no more than a few metres.[14] Hopper [24] actually regards this class of system as one of a number of categories that make up LANs, where polling and crossbar switch strategies are utilized, but does not develop this class any further (see Fig.1). Tanenbaum [3] also examines shared memory systems with other LANs, whereas Weitzman [25] regards them as one of six multiminicomputer architectures differing in degrees of coupling and centralization, but not specifically in the context of LANs.

The reader should note that most discussions of LANs are not so much concerned with shared memory systems, as with ring and contention systems and sometimes PABXs, where the geographical dispersion is often much greater than a few metres.

Shared memory systems find application where there is a requirement for high data rates and a high level of availability. In order to satisfy these requirements, simultaneous memory accesses by the interconnected processors is accomplished by dividing up the shared memory into a number of separate units (modules).

The interconnection of the processors, memory modules, and peripherals may take different forms and is the subject of what follows.

Probably the simplest method for interconnecting processors to allow access to a number of memory modules is by means of a bit serial or parallel common bus. (In a parallel bus, specific lines may be allocated for data memory addresses and control signals.) Nevertheless, the bus, like the memory modules and the peripherals, is also a common resource and as only one processor may use it at any one time, various control strategies are implemented to resolve the competition amongst the processors. Generally, such control strategies for sharing common memory are grouped together under the heading of *time-shared bus* (Fig. 4a).

The problem of sharing common memory sometimes means that one processor assumes the responsibility for the system-wide coordination of resource utilization and it is this aspect which results in this class of system tending towards a centralized architecture.

The use of a specific processor to arbitrate amongst the competing processors for the use of a common bus is one such approach, but connection to a *central arbiter* can assume different degrees of centralization [3,25].

One such form involves the connection of each processor to the central arbiter by two wires—one dedicated to requests, the other dedicated to granting requests by the central arbiter. Clearly, in terms of system growth, this implementation is inflexible as there will be a limit to the number of processors that can be attached to the central arbiter.

An alternative form of centralized arbitration involves *polling* the competing processors in a particular order after receiving a request from one processor for the use of the bus [3,24]. This differs from the previous implementation in that the processors are attached in parallel to one request line and one grant line of the central arbiter.

Daisy chaining is another variation, and differs from the last centralized architecture in that the parallel grant line is replaced by a serial grant line, which interconnects the central arbiter to the other processors. Hence, on granting a request, the arbiter merely forwards the grant to the first processor to which it is connected. The grant is then forwarded in a serial manner by each subsequent processor until it reaches the intended processor.

Of course, it is not necessary to employ a centralized control strategy on a common bus at all, but to employ some time division multiplexing strategy amongst all the processors attached to the system in a decentralized manner. It is this fact that makes it problematic as to whether shared memory systems

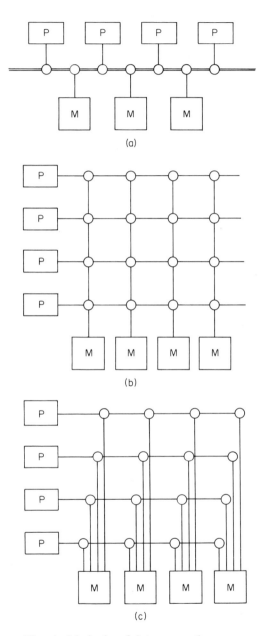

Fig. 4. Methods of interconnecting processors and memory: (a) time-shared bus,
(b) crosspoint switch, and (c) multiported
memory.

should be positioned nearer to centralized systems than some 'loosely coupled' systems. The fact that a common pool of memory is shared probably justifies this position as this tends to limit system flexibility.

Clearly, the use of a common bus does not allow simultaneous transfers between processors and memory modules. Increasing the number of buses, where each processor, memory module, and peripheral unit has a separate bus, results in an interconnection in the form of a matrix (grid) and is referred to as a *crosspoint switch* [3] or a *crossbar switch* [24,25] (see Fig. 4b). The switch is responsible for the resolution of requests from processors and directing transfer requests between the processors and the memory modules.

Multiported shared memory systems [3,25] (Fig. 4c) represent a distributed solution to a number of processors accessing a number of memory modules. No central arbiter or switch exists here. Instead, multiple dedicated buses interconnect processors, memory modules, and peripherals. Each memory module and peripheral unit is directly connected to each processor and thus the number of ports on each is equal to the number of processors. A control strategy for resolving simultaneous accesses to the memory modules from two or more processors is often achieved by allocating priorities to the ports on the memory modules. Thus, this architecture is constrained by the number of ports available on the processors, memory modules, and peripheral units, and this does not permit growth of the system.

4.2 Decentralized Control Strategies

These are strategies or approaches which are felt to be more decentralized in nature. Centralized control strategies tend to have a central controller (usually a minicomputer or a mainframe) which makes the appropriate circuit switch in a LCSN, or which receives, stores, and routes messages in LMSNs and LPSNs, etc. No such powerful central controller exists in the decentralized control strategies. Control functions are needed and do exist on rings and contention networks, but the approach of dealing with these control functions is much more distributed than in the centralized control strategies. This, it is hoped, will be made clear by what follows.

4.2.1 Rings

The ring architecture (Fig. 5) is a distributed architecture with minimal connectivity and a topology of two links connected to every node. Most rings are operated in a unidirectional manner and are distinct from loops, which are generally considered to have a centralized control strategy [11]. (Joyce, however, regards rings and loops to be equivalent [14].)

As can be seen from Table 5 a number of control strategies are observable. Some simple descriptions of the strategies will be offered here.

Clark *et al.* regard ring control strategies as falling into two types: those that

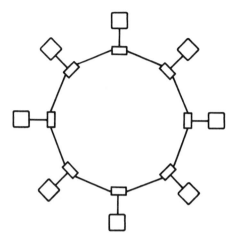

Fig. 5. Ring structure.

require permission to transmit (daisy chain, control token, and circulating slots) and those where the network is 'broken' (register insertion) [7].

Daisy chain networks employ dedicated wires to pass information from one node to the next. A node must receive the appropriate control information (through the daisy chain network) before it is allowed to transmit. (Compare daisy chaining to a time-shared memory bus.)

Control tokens are special bit patterns transmitted over the regular data channel. This type of ring is the oldest and still the most popular and requires the seizure and removal of the token by a station prior to transmission. After this station has completed transmission, it relinquishes the control token and then the next station downstream will seize the token and begin transmitting. Thus, the control token is passed around the ring in a round-robin fashion and only that station which is in possession of the token can transmit. In this sense the control strategy is not dissimilar to that of 'hub polling' mentioned earlier. Here, however, there is no master station directly controlling transmission. Thus, a station will never experience contention when transmitting, but concurrent use of the ring bandwidth by two or more stations, even in non-overlapping parts of the ring, is not catered for.

Weitzman [25] considers two methods for passing on the control token. One method allows the control token to be passed on only after the queue of messages in a station interface have been transmitted. The other method passes the control token on after the station, currently in possession of the token, has transmitted a message and all other messages, queueing for transmission, are ignored.

The performance characteristics of the two methods are as follows: the first results in greater latency before transmission because of the similar delays incurred by transmitting the queues of other messages or other stations around the ring. Thus, the first method is characterized by longer average and maximum message queue lengths. However, once in possession of the token the total time for message transmission is much less than when the second scheme is employed, which displays the converse characteristics, i.e. shorter queue lengths, but increased total message transmission time.

The use of control tokens is not restricted to physical rings, but also to 'logical rings'. Here, the control token holds the address of the next host node in a sequence of stations which had been established when the system was implemented. (The reader is directed to Miller and Thompson [26] for a discussion of the issues involved in 'logical rings', i.e. the token bus, using the control token as a media access protocol, but should note that the problems of token buses are equally applicable to token rings.)

Because the media access method of token passing is independent of the LAN topology, this has contributed to its inclusion in the current standards efforts. (The issues of standards will be discussed in more detail in Part II.)

Circulating slots are marked full or empty and when a station wishes to transmit it merely waits for an empty slot, marks it as full and puts the data in the slot. Packets must be small enough to fit in the slot in contrast to the token and connection rings which support packets of arbitrarily large sizes [18]. This strategy is not completely decentralized as one node must generate the slot patterns [7].

A variant of the circulating slots control strategy involves a 'train' of messages travelling around the ring. Each station removes any messages it has originated from the train and also scans for any messages specifically addressed to it, copying them off and marking them as read. A special control token or 'caboose' signifies the end of the train and the station can then insert any new messages immediately before the 'caboose'. By the time the train returns these new messages should have been moved to the front (owing to the removal of messages previously in front of them) where they too can be removed [27].

Register insertion is a control strategy involving the insertion of a message to be transmitted into a shift register [3]. When the network is idle or at a convenient point between two adjacent messages, the message to be sent is shifted out onto the network whilst any arriving message is shifted into the register behind the message being transmitted. Delay encountered with this control strategy is variable depending on the number of messages currently being sent around the ring.

4.2.2 Contention networks

Contention networks represent the final class of LANs to be considered. This simple control strategy involves the situation in which stations compete for use of the transmission medium. Any station wishing to transmit does so, but as there is no priority nothing prevents transmissions from various stations colliding and messages becoming garbled or lost. If the traffic on the LAN is low, then the number of collisions and subsequent retransmissions will be tolerably small.

Various contention control strategies, some employing collision detection, have been well summarized by Tanenbaum [3]. Carrier sense networks, as he refers to them, can support different cable topologies, e.g. linear, spine, tree, and segmented (Fig. 6), but not rings.

Significant improvements can be gained by employing particular contention control strategies to minimize the number of collisions occurring on the network. One of the most common strategies is 'listen before talking' (LBT) or, as it is more generally referred to, *carrier sense multiple access* (CSMA). CSMA involves stations listening to the carrier (channel) for transmissions and then acting accordingly. If a station wants to transmit and detects the carrier idle, it may transmit. If, on the other hand, the carrier is busy, the station waits for a random period of time before attempting to transmit again.

Carrier sense multiple access-collision detection (CSMA-CD) is an improvement on CSMA and is employed by Ethernet to which part of the next chapter

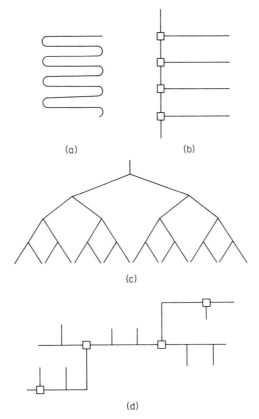

Fig. 6. (a) Linear, (b) spine, (c) tree, and (d) segmented cable topologies.

will be devoted. Briefly, this control strategy greatly reduces the amount of bandwidth wasted when collisions occur. This is achieved by all stations monitoring the cable during their own transmission and if a collision is detected then transmission is terminated immediately. The stations then 'back-off' for a random amount of time and try again if no other station has begun transmission in the intervening period. This strategy is sometimes referred to as 'listen while talking' (LWT).

Once a station has possession of the channel under CSMA-CD no collisions can occur but as they still can occur during the contention period, collisions can degrade performance significantly. Some control strategies resolve the contention without any collisions at all. *Contention-free* protocols include bit-map protocols, binary countdown, and multilevel-multiaccess protocols [3].

The two most important performance parameters, delay under light load and channel efficiency at high load, determine the relative performance of CSMA-CD and contention-free protocols. The former functions well under conditions of light load and the latter performs best at high load.

Limited contention protocols attempt to combine the best properties of the contention and collision-free protocols by dividing the stations into groups and allowing only one member of each group to contend for channel utilization. Examples of such protocols include the adaptive tree walk protocol and the urn protocol.

4.3   An Evolutionary Taxonomy

Thus far, this chapter has been concerned with classifications which are based on the topology and control strategy of LANs. This approach is valuable in that it lends itself to an appraisal of LANs. Hence a determination of their required features is possible. But this is not the only taxonomic method possible.

Freeman and Thurber [1] have classified LANs according to the evolutionary context of the system. Some LANs have evolved as an experiment in distributed processing while others have evolved out of a need to improve system usage, to extend communication capabilities, or to provide more memory at reasonable cost.

Seven categories are identified in the taxonomy developed by Freeman and Thurber (Fig. 7). The major LANs are listed for each category, but it should be noted that the original reference is far more extensive. In this classification, it is possible for a system to move from one category to another during the process of its evolution. The taxonomy covers a gamut of LANs: implementations which are presently incomplete, working LANs, and those commercially available.

Consider the Ethernet as an example. This LAN was originally conceived as an experiment in distributed processing, but in the past few years multiple Ethernets have been interconnected to avoid systems bottlenecks. The Ethernet is now classified under 'Existing System Improvement'. Currently, Fibernet is

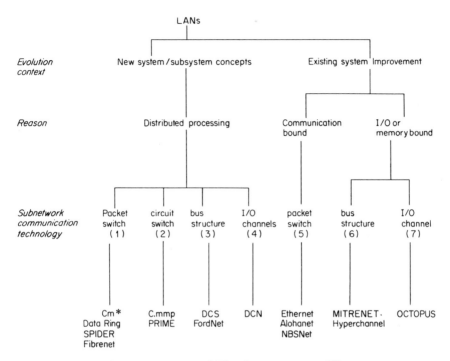

Fig. 7. Freeman and Thurber taxonomy [1].

being developed in which distributed processing concepts associated with Ethernet are being implemented with a fibre optic carrier and consequently appears under 'New System Concepts'.

Chapter 5
The Cambridge Ring and the Ethernet

The aim of this chapter is to describe briefly the Cambridge Ring and the Ethernet. Particular attention will be given to how they differ from one another.

The rationale for comparing these two LANs and not some others is essentially twofold. First, there currently exists a debate in the field of LANs concerning the relative merits of the Cambridge Ring and the Ethernet.[15] Secondly, as a consequence of this argument, many LAN products available have tended to adopt Cambridge Ring or Ethernet technology.[16]

5.1 The Cambridge Ring

5.1.1 Ring hardware

The Cambridge Digital Communication Ring [9,18,24,28] (Fig. 8) operates at 10 MHz and signals are transmitted along two twisted pairs of wires.[17] It is possible to accommodate up to 256 stations where the separation between repeaters cannot exceed 100 m. The repeaters themselves are powered directly from the ring and must operate reliably whether connected to a station or not. Power is injected at a number of independent points by power supply units (PSUs).

Each node on the ring consists of a *repeater*, a *station*, and an *access box* (Fig. 9a) [7][18]. Each station is fully duplex enabling transmission and reception to occur concurrently and independently. The number of bits delay on each station is approximately 1.5 bits and the minimum ring delay is approximately five microseconds.

There is also one unique station in the ring called a *monitor station*. Its responsibilities include establishing slot structure during turn on, monitoring the ring, clearing lost packets, and the accumulation of error statistics. Immediately preceding the monitor station is an error logging station which uses a normal station and receives packets containing error information sent from active ring stations and the monitor station.

A number of access boxes have been developed and their complexity varies according to the speed of the attached host and the level of buffering needed.

34

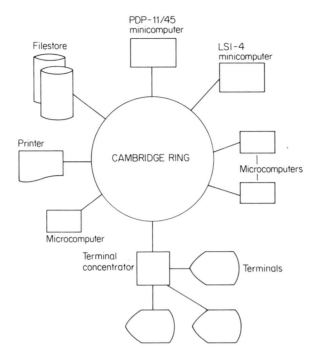

Fig. 8. A simplified Cambridge Ring.

There are three types of access boxes (interfaces) available and these differ in complexity according to one of three procedures which allow communication between the access box and its attached host.

The simplest of the three types is the *polled* interface which is suitable for the attachment of microcomputers. Here, hosts are simply connected to the data bus and address bus in the interface. Depending on the microcomputer system, some connection to a combination of the control bus lines may also be necessitated.

These microprocessor based interfaces contain a program which implements a polling algorithm where periodically the microprocessor will ask each host attached to its data bus whether it requires service. In practice, this may probably involve testing a flag set by the host. The predictability of the order in which attached hosts will be polled is a major programming advantage, but the software overhead incurred by polling all hosts, some of which may not require service, may result in an intolerable waste of processor time.

Whenever polling interfaces do not provide an adequate response time, *interrupt* interfaces are employed. This second type of interface is so called because the attached hosts request service by sending a message along an interrupt line to the interface's microprocessor. Two or more attached hosts may send interrupts simultaneously and thus priorities may be assigned to

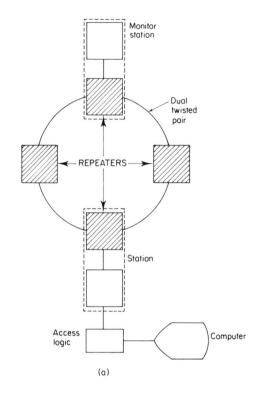

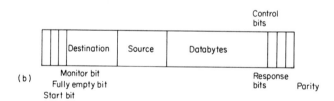

Fig. 9. (a) Repeaters and (b) packet structure.

resolve this contention. Once the microprocessor in the interface has received the interrupt and determined its origin, the program it was executing is suspended and the interrupt serviced by an interrupt handling routine. Interrupt interfaces are usually employed when a real-time response is required and is the simplest for the attachment of a minicomputer.

Clearly, a software overhead is still incurred every time an attached host interrupts the executing program. The implementation of these interrupt handlers in hardware to accelerate the process represents the third type of interface.

Direct memory access (DMA) interfaces provide an even faster service than the interrupt interfaces. An interrupt is sent to a DMA instead of the microprocessor of the interface. The DMA suspends the microprocessor and assumes control of the interface automatically providing high-speed block transfers between the attached host and the memory in the interface. In the Cambridge Ring, this could involve buffering a number of ring minipackets and writing them back to store in one block. Such an interface has been developed based on the 8X300 microprocessor.

5.1.2 Modus operandi

The Cambridge Ring was originally designed on the register insertion principle. Here, the packet to be transmitted is placed in a shift register and inserted in series with the ring at an appropriate moment. As the delay in register insertion and thus transmission is, at the most, one packet time, all nodes share the bandwidth equally. This prevents one particular station 'hogging' the LAN.

The adoption of the 'circulating empty slot' in its simplest form did not relieve the ring of the 'hogging' problem. The solution was to mark each packet as 'empty' only after it had passed its original source, i.e. after one complete revolution. Both approaches performed similarly, but the latter was favoured as the interaction at each node was minimized, thereby improving the reliability of the system.

Before continuing with a description of the use of the 'circulating slots' for transmission in the Cambridge Ring, a brief description of the packet structure (Fig. 9b) is provided.

The packet structure itself was chosen to maximize timing tolerance and minimize delay at the transmitter and receiver. The first bit is always one and is immediately followed by a bit indicating whether the slot is full or empty. The control bit is used by the monitor station to mark, as empty, packets which would circulate indefinitely owing to an error in the full/empty bit. Four eight-bit bytes now follow: the first two are used for the destination and source addresses respectively and the last two for data. Finally, there are two control bits for acknowledgement purposes and a parity bit for ring maintenance.

When any station is ready to transmit, it awaits the arrival of the next slot. The full/empty bit is read whilst simultaneously a one is written at the output. If the full/empty bit equals zero, a packet can be transmitted, but if it equals one, then the slot is already occupied and the algorithm is rejected until the arrival of the next slot. Hence transmission is delayed until an empty slot is found. But once found, however, transmission occurs rapidly.[19] In the event that a station recognizes the destination address of the transmitted packet as its own, the control packets are set 'on the fly', to indicate accepted, busy or rejected. The packet then returns to its source where it is marked 'empty', but if it is returned marked 'busy', immediate retransmission is prohibited. The additional delay incurred here depends on ring loading and approximates to the time to acquire the next empty slot. If retransmissions are attempted, the extra delay is increased to about 16 times the original delay.

Each station 'knows' the total number of slots in the ring and thus empties its own transmitted packet by simply counting the number of packets that pass it and then clearing the full/empty bit.

5.1.3 Error detection

The source or monitor station usually detects errors within one ring delay. The parity bit, positioned at the end of the packet, is continually computed by every station. An increased delay is avoided by writing parity and simultaneously sensing it. Hence, as each station inserts parity, any fault that occurs must have arisen since the last active station.

The scheme also allows ring breaks to be detected. When there are no data at the input, the phase-locked loop at each repeater continually operates at the centre of its frequency range. This is interpreted as a string of zeros and the station sends a repeated fault message packet to which all other repeaters synchronize. In the event that the ring is completely severed and the transmission of data impossible, the forward data path is used to send fault localizing messages.

5.2 The Ethernet

5.2.1 Configuration

The Ethernet [3,4,11,14,29–31] consists of a coaxial cable whose configuration is by the connection of a number of independent terminals via an interface to a transceiver, which is in turn connected to the transmission medium (Fig. 10).

The topology is that of an unrooted tree, in the sense that there is a unique path between any pair of stations. Any station wishing to join an Ethernet taps into the ether at the nearest convenient point via a transceiver without any disruption to the ongoing network. Extensions of the cable from any of its points is possible by the use of repeaters, which operate on a bit-by-bit basis with essentially no delay in the repeater, or on the store-and-forward basis with address filtering.[20]

Thus, the Ethernet is conferred with considerable topological flexibility permitting the interconnection of one or more cable segments. Each segment can be up to 500 m long where separate segments can be joined by a repeater connected between two transceivers in each cable.

Where cable segments are more than 100 m apart, a point-to-point link between the two repeaters can be used to link two segments at distances up to 100 m. The maximum total length between any two transceivers on the network is 2500 m (1500 m of coaxial cable plus 1000 m of point-to-point link).

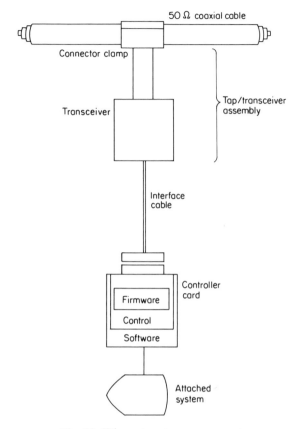

Fig. 10. Ethernet system components.

5.2.2 Interfaces

Speed conversions between all stations are intrinsic to the Ethernet interfaces as all transmission within the network occurs at a different speed from the speed of the terminals. In order to prevent buffer overflow and the resulting loss of data, flow control must be exercised.

The original Ethernet design differentiated between the *interface* and the *controller*.[21] When implemented, interfaces were designed separately for each type of station, with the controller resident in the station as low-level firmware or software. Subsequent implementations have adopted the combination of the interface and controller functions into a separate buffered device between the station and the transceiver.

5.2.3 Modus Operandi

All stations on the Ethernet monitor the cable during their own transmission and, upon detection of a collision, transmission is aborted. The employ-

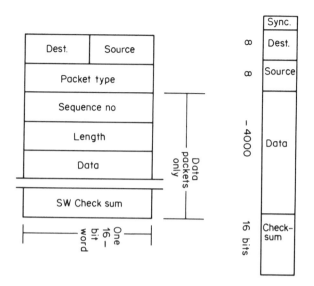

Fig. 11. Ethernet frame.

ment of the datagram concept and the control of links by contention arbitration and collision detection greatly reduces the amount of bandwidth wasted on colliding packets. This precludes any Ethernet configuration in which more than one path exists between two points. The transmission would interfere with itself, repeatedly arriving at its intended destination after having travelled various paths of different lengths.

A typical transmitted Ethernet frame is shown in Fig. 11. The first 16 bits of all Ethernet packets represent the destination and source station addresses which are interpreted by the interface. A software convention requires that the second 16 bits contain the packet type. The Ethernet file transport protocol uses five packet types: data, ack, abort, end, and end reply. The packet type is followed by a 16 bit sequence number and optionally by some 16 bit datawords and finally a 16 bit software checksum word [6].

Operating experience seems to indicate that the emphasis on distributed control and minimization of the shared components of the communication systems has resulted in a high level of reliability. Installation and maintenance have been satisfactory and the flexibility afforded by station interconnection and broadcast packet switching has encouraged the development of numerous computer networking and multiprocessor applications.

5.3   A Comparison of the Cambridge Ring and the Ethernet

The reader is referred to Tables 6 and 7.

TABLE 6
A brief comparison of the Cambridge Ring and the Ethernet specifications

Physical layer	Cambridge Ring	Ethernet
Data rate	10 Mbps (repeaters)	10 Mbps
	n/a	
Max. station separation		2.5 km
Max. no. of stations	256	1024
Medium	Two twisted pairs baseband signalling	Shielded coaxial baseband signalling
Topology	Ring	Branching unrooted tree (bus)
Maximum cable segment	100 m (repeaters)	500 m
Maximum transceivers per cable segment	n/a	100
Maximum total cable length along longest path between two transceivers	n/a	1500 m
Maximum total coaxial cable length between any two transceivers	n/a	1500 m

TABLE 7
A brief comparison of the Cambridge Ring and the Ethernet (cont'd)

Data link layer	Cambridge Ring	Ethernet [30]
Link control procedure	Byte stream protocol built upon basic ring block protocol (circulating slot)	Fully distributed peer protocol with statistical contention resolution (CSMA–CD)
Message protocol	2 bytes of data	Variable size frame best effort delivery
Packet length	38–40 bits	68–1522 bytes
Packet format	Start of packet 1 bit Full/empty 1 bit Monitor station 1 bit Destination 8 bits Source 8 bits Data 16 bits Control 2 bits Parity 1 bit	Packet preamble 32 bits Destination device 48 bits Source device 48 bits Packet types 16 bits Data field 45–1500 bytes Checksum 32 bits

The Cambridge Ring does not readily fit in with the ISO OSI reference model at all. The basic block protocol in fact, includes the physical layer and overlaps into the data link layer. The byte stream protocol occupies the data link layer and also part of the network layer. The remainder of the network layer is occupied by the transport service byte stream protocol, which does not occupy any position in the transport layer.

5.3.1 Reliability issues

Although one of the prime motivations for the adoption of the ring and bus topologies was to eliminate the potential reliability problem with a central node, e.g. a star, these alternatives are not without their drawbacks.

The contention control strategy of the Ethernet appears to possess an inherent reliability advantage over the ring control strategies. In the latter, there exists some entity (a control token or explicit signal in the wire) which passes from node to node, indicating which node currently has the right to transmit. Because the destruction of this entity is possible, e.g. a noise burst on the transmission medium, any ring control strategy must possess the capability of restarting by the regeneration of the permission to transmit. In the case of a completely decentralized control strategy, it is difficult to ascertain that the entity has been definitely lost and it is problematic to determine which node should be responsible for its regeneration. One solution is to employ a contention system among the various nodes, but in the Cambridge Ring the monitor station provides a centralized restart mechanism.

In contrast, any transient failure in the Ethernet is treated as a collision, as the effects are exactly the same. However, the contention control requires the destination to detect the garbled message and also be capable of requesting retransmission, if the source has failed to discover that its original message was garbled. Thus, mechanisms which ensure reliable recovery must be provided by higher-level protocols, but this would be required irrespective of the LAN control strategy.

Another consideration on the question of reliability stems from the respective natures of the Cambridge Ring and the Ethernet. The former requires each node to be able to remove a message selectively from the ring or retransmit to the next node. Thus, each node needs an active repeater, as it participates in the implementation of the control strategy.

As a consequence, there may be a significant amount of logic at each node, whose failure would disable the ring. Thus the ring can be no more reliable than its repeaters. The reliability of these repeaters must be ensured with a dependable power supply (PSUs) to minimize the probability of failure. This is achieved by the repeaters being powered from the ring. An alternative technique is the provision of a relay at each repeater that can mechanically remove it from the network in the event of failure, including local power failure.

Compare this with the passive medium of the Ethernet. Each node senses the ether and requires message generation at each node. Failure of a node is tolerable as long as it is in a manner that presents a high impedance to the bus.

Practical experience related to these LANs is not extensive, but the indications are that both may be made relatively error free.[22] One significant factor in LANs is hardware reliability, in particular the quality and care of the engineering design. This has been considered in detail by Clark *et al.* who conclude there are certain design problems in the bus contention which do not arise in the ring.[23] The comparison so far seems to favour the Ethernet, primarily because node failure would disable the Cambridge Ring whilst the Ethernet node must fail in a particular manner. However, consider the catastrophic disruption of the transmission medium, e.g. a lightning strike or errant cross-connection to the power lines. This would result in the inevitable destruction of all electronic components connected to the medium. In the Cambridge Ring, such components would mean one set of line drivers and one set of receivers, but for the Ethernet, every node would be damaged. Clearly, both LANs would suffer disablement but the Ethernet would take longer to repair.

5.3.2 Performance issues

A comparative evaluation of the performance of the Ethernet and the token passing ring has concluded that the former functions well under light loads, but with increasing traffic loads time is wasted in collision avoidance [34][24].

According to Mok and Ward [34], in the Ethernet, as the cable length increases a further deterioration in performance occurs as the result of a longer contention interval. The ring, supposedly, maintains high system throughput even under very heavy loads. However, Shoch and Hupp assert that the comparison made by Mok and Ward is incorrect. They claim that resolution of collisions is very quick when using the Ethernet control strategy and thus throughput, even under heavy loads, remains very high [35].

Blair and Sheperd [36] have concluded that the minipacket protocol employed by the Cambridge Ring causes higher expected delays compared to the Ethernet for most configurations. However, if the LAN size increases, the performance of the Ethernet is subject to degradation, but the Cambridge Ring remains relatively unaffected. This is due to an increase in the collision window (contention interval) in the Ethernet, whereas the ring compensates for the increased ring delay by the accommodation of more circulating slots.

The effect of increasing message sizes revealed that the performance of the Ethernet is superior to that of the Cambridge Ring. This is attributable to two factors. First, fixed overheads decrease in proportion to the increased packet length and, secondly, the message transmission time increases relative to the collision window. Thus, the significance of time wasted on collisions declines [36].

The fact that the Cambridge Ring maintained its efficiency level for the message sizes simulated was not unexpected, as all messages may be decomposed into minipackets of a fixed size.

A simple comparison of the variance of the delays for the two LAN approaches showed the Ethernet to have higher variance at all load levels. This is because the binary exponential back-off (BEB) algorithm employed by the Ethernet increases the retransmission delay with the increasing number of collisions. Thus, stations which have attempted to retransmit several times are delayed much longer than a station which is about to attempt transmitting for the first time. This has led to the proposal of other algorithms, some of which are more adaptive in nature than the BEB [37] (see Appendix A).

In contrast, the Cambridge Ring can guarantee transmission time to not exceed a certain duration. Simply, this maximum time is relative to the number of stations and the number of minipackets of the ring.

The important features of performance in the Cambridge Ring are its high bandwidth and its very low error rate (1 error in 5×10^{11} bits) [28]. The lower error rate is significant as this allows protocols to be simple. Hence, as faults occur infrequently and bandwidth is not such a precious resource, simplification of lower-level protocols is possible as they need not be so concerned with the transmission of correct packets should a fault occur. Instead, this can be handled by higher-level protocols which would merely request that the packet be retransmitted (repetition). The bandwidth itself is a strong function of ring size and in particular the number of circulating slots. It should be noted that doubling the basic data rate (10–20 Mbps) does not double the point-to-point performance (see Appendix B).

Increasing the number of data bytes per packet is one method for improving performance under consideration at Cambridge University Computer Laboratory. Also being considered are certain enhancements. The inclusion of a number of user-regulated control bits which would also serve to identify control packets (marked by a non-unique bit pattern) is one such enhancement. Another is a broadcast feature where each station recognizes a particular minipacket destination address. Such options are being scrutinzed and may be included in a new version of the ring based in LSI.

5.3.3 Concluding comments on the comparison

The ring is the simplest of the LANs in terms of the number of nodes and links and has no routing problems. The bus possesses the same amount of routing hardware as the ring and routing is straightforward despite having more links.

Although the relative merits of their respective performances will continue to be debated, it has been shown that both possess similar performance characteristics and that delay is related to the number of nodes in the LAN [38]. The ring has the largest theoretical delay but in contention networks errors are assumed to occur frequently. Rings can be made relatively error free, but in the Ethernet error occurrence is assumed to be frequent, necessitating powerful error detection facilities [24].

On the issue of practical suitability, the Ethernet was not designed for use in hostile environments nor where a real-time response needs to be guaranteed. Thus, the Ethernet would be unsuitable for process control or other real-time applications. But in office environments where the Ethernet has been used for the transmission of data and text, the bandwidth, although far from being fully utilized, has been adequate. It must be borne in mind that its random nature of transmission has made it unsuitable for voice communication. The

Cambridge Ring, however, is now handling voice transmission which is achieved by dial servers aiding telephone-telephone communication or telephone-processor communication in the system [39].

In conclusion, both LAN approaches have their strengths and weaknesses but it should be clear that neither of the two has any specific feature or facility which makes it greatly superior to the other. It is for this very reason that the issue of standards has been so difficult and that none of the major standards agencies have come down in favour of either an Ethernet or a Cambridge Ring standard. (The issue of standards will receive considerable attention in Part II of this book.) No doubt the debate over the relative merits of both approaches will continue unabated. It is hoped that this book's treatment of the comparison will help the reader appreciate the myriad issues surrounding LAN assessment.

PART II:
PRODUCTS,
EVALUATION,
and DEVELOPMENTS

Chapter 6

LAN Products

This section briefly describes some LAN products which are currently available. The products chosen for inclusion are felt to be representative of what is currently on the market. It must be noted that the list of products is in no way exhaustive.

Treatment of the various products is, by necessity, uneven. This is because information available on the various products varies considerably. Some products, because of their age and commercial availability and use, have a great deal of information pertaining to them. Others, which are perhaps more recent and are just now becoming commercially available, have produced much less information. Thus, LAN product treatment in this book may not be as consistent and even as one might like. Nevertheless, an attempt has been made to integrate the various materials available and present them in a manner which makes LAN comparison possible—although difficult.

Product descriptions have been written to follow a broad outline of: product architecture, hardware, software, costs, and miscellaneous.

For simplicity, a distinction has been made between ring-based products and non-ring products despite the shortcomings of the approach and thus the chapter has been divided accordingly. Within the ring products there are two subdivisions. The first subdivision concerns 'Cambridge Ring LANs' and the second concerns 'Other Ring LANs' which employ other network access protocols instead of circulating slots. Within the non-ring products, there are a number of subdivisions. The first of these subdivisions concerns 'Single Vendor Supported LANs'. The second outlines some typical 'Multivendor Supported LANs'. The third and fourth subdivisions are respectively concerned with 'Broadband LANs' and 'High-Speed LANs' (see Appendix C for list of LAN vendors).

6.1 Ring Products

The reader is referred to Table 8.

TABLE 8
Ring Products.

	Vendor(s)	Media access/ packet size	Data rate	Medium	Number of stations	Range	Interfaces	Comments
6.1.1 Cambridge Ring products								
6.1.1.1 Cambridge Ring	Acorn Computers Ltd	Circulating slots/ 40-bit packet	10 Mbps	two twisted pairs	256 (8 bit address)	≤300 m between stations	Z80 polled interface, Acorn (6502) (interrupt), PDP-11 Unibus (interrupt), PDP-11 (DMA), LSI-11 Q-bus (DMA), LSI/4 (DMA), Nova (interrupt)	Capability to handle voice is claimed. Enhanced 20 MHz available. TTL technology.
6.1.1.2 Data Ring	Toltec Ltd	Circulating slots/ 40 bit packet	10 Mbps	twin pair cable	256 (8 bit address)	unspecified	PDP-11 Unibus (interrupt), PDP-11 (DMA), LSI-11 (DMA), LSI/4 (interrupt), RS232, S-100, IEEE 488	Future developments include –ULA-2 chips on a small printed circuit board –voice communication
6.1.1.3 Polynet	Logica VTS Ltd	Circulating slots/ 38 or 40 bit packets	10 Mbps	triple twisted pairs	256 (8 bit address)	≤100 m between stations	PDP-11 Unibus (DMA), LSI-11 Q-bus (DMA), Intel Multibus	LSI chips to perform some mode functions in future. Logica have an in-house system installed
6.1.1.4 TransRing 2000	SEEL	Circulating slots/ 38 or 40 bit packets	10 Mbps	two twisted pairs	256 (8 bit address)	unspecified	Unibus (interrupt + DMA), Q-bus (interrupt + DMA), S-100 A 16 terminal concentrator is also available	

	Company	Access method/packet	Speed	Medium	Number of devices	Distance	Machine interfaces	Notes
6.1.1.5 Planet	Racal-Milgo Ltd	Circulating slots/42 bit packet	10 Mbps	dual coaxial cable	256	unspecified	RS232C	Some back-up provided by duplication of medium. Re-routing the signal in the opposite direction along the other cable on either side of the break
6.1.2 *Other ring products*								
6.1.2.1 SILK	Hasler (GB) Ltd	Register insertion/(32–128 bits)	16.896 Mbps	Coaxial cable (75 Ω)	150 LBLs × 7 = 1050 devices	200 m (LBL–LBL)	X.21, V.24 machine interfaces not specified	Voice is handled on system –through 'braiding' integrity
6.1.2.2 Xinet/ Xibus	Xionics Ltd	Circulating slots (each intelligent socket has one slot)/256 bytes	~ 1 Mbps	10 twisted pairs (multi-core cable)	4095 addresses on Xinet (400 terminals per Xinet) 100 terminals	not specified	IBM 370, 3033, 3270 protocol. ICL 2960, Univac 1100, Honeywell Level 6, Vydec + Philips WPs	Xibus can accommodate up to 16 Xinet rings. Data, voice, and image processing provided. Provide real-time voice conversations with voice annotation of text –duplication of all hardware and software modules
6.1.2.3 DOMAIN	Apollo Computer (UK) Ltd/ Apollo Computer Inc.	Token passing/ variable	12 Mbps	coaxial	unspecified	1000 m between nodes	Apollo computers only. IEEE Multibus interface also available	Each computational node can handle graphics and may include 33 or 66 Mbyte disk. UNIX-like command environment. Each user has own dedicated processor

TABLE 8 (contd)
Ring Products.

	Vendor(s)	Media access/ packet size	Data rate	Medium	Number of stations	Range	Interfaces	Comments
6.1.2.4 ODR-1	Syscon Ltd	TDM (central controller and 15 slaves)	500 kbps	fibre optic	16	25–40 m between stations (3000 m separation is possible)	RS232C	ODR-2 dual-channel system. Bandwidth sufficient to support speech
6.1.2.5 Clearway	Real Time Development Ltd	Analogous to register insertion	35 kbaud	coaxial cable	99 stations	500 m	RS232C	Network handles graphics + alpha-numeric data. 50 stations considered practical limit
6.1.2.6 Multilink	Hawker Siddeley Dynamics Engineering Ltd	unspecified	19.2 kbaud	twisted pair	125 Multilink station units	total length 400 km station–station ≤1 km	RS232C	
6.1.2.7 Pronet	Proteon Associates Inc.	token passing/ variable	10 Mbps	twisted pair, coaxial, fibre optic, microwave	255 nodes	'several thousand feet'	DEC PDP-11s LSI-11s	Directed at Unibus and Q-bus computers

6.1.1 Cambridge Ring products

6.1.1.1 The Cambridge Ring

The Cambridge Ring, produced by Acorn Computers Ltd, Cambridge (UK), utilizes the circulating slot strategy [40]. The ring is constructed using TTL technology and operates at 10 MHz. Each station is fully duplex enabling transmission and reception to occur simultaneously and concurrently. A 3-bit delay exists at each repeater and the minimum ring delay is five microseconds.

A number of different access boxes are available and their complexity depends upon the speed of the host and the level of buffering required. Polled interfaces are suitable for microprocessor attachment, interrupt interfaces for minicomputers, and DMA interfaces where high bandwidth is required.

The cost of a node and 200 m of connecting cable is approximately £300, but this does not include the cost of the access boxes (interfaces). The interfaces vary in price according to their complexity. For instance, a simple polled interface costs approximately £50, but a DEC LSI-11 Q-bus DMA interface which is suitable for handling the basic block protocol costs approximately £3270.

Gateways interconnecting two rings can also be constructed by wiring a computer with two access boxes. Ring utilization in adverse environments is also possible using screened cable or fibre optics. It is claimed that speech transmission is possible on the ring where several hundred telephones in normal use can be supported although this is not substantiated. An enhanced version of the ring operating at 20 MHz will be available in the future and the company is developing even faster systems (100 Mbps), but when and if these will be marketed is uncertain. Systems of such data rates will provide the capacity necessary for video and facsimile transmission.

6.1.1.2 Data Ring

Data Ring, produced by Toltec Ltd, is another 'circulating slot' Cambridge Ring [41,42]. The company can supply a full range of software for Data Ring, most of which is written in the high-level language BCPL. This can run under the native operating system or under TROUT, Toltec's own portable packet-oriented operating system also written in BCPL.

Drivers and handlers make up the basic software. These control data transfer to and from a given station, implement the basic block protocol (BBP) and maintain a list of reception requests relating to port numbers. For particular devices, these functions may be assigned to the access logic. The single shot protocol (SSP) implemented is a combination of transmitted and received basic blocks. This is the fundamental unit of conversation for standard interfaces to the ring handler. File transfer between dissimilar operating systems is effected using the byte stream protocol (BSP).[25]

A repeater unit and 200 m of cable costs approximately £390. Interfaces range from £400 to £1100 for a DMA interface based on the 8X300 microprocessor.

A wide variety of applications is claimed, covering all industrial and commercial communications requirements, e.g. process control, test equipment, office automation, and management information. A file server which possesses all the necessary software and files allows the implementation of shared logic word processing. The output can be through shared printers connected through terminal concentrators in a manner similar to the terminals themselves. A 'gateway' machine also allows geographically separate networks to communicate with each other.

6.1.1.3 *Polynet*

In this third Cambridge Ring product, Polynet (Logica VTS Ltd.(UK)) [43] (Fig. 12), two forms of cabling can be employed. First, it is possible to configure a ring by installing a set of wall sockets and interconnecting them using triple twisted pair cable. A plug resembling a telephone jack plug is used to connect Polynet components at convenient points and the nodes themselves may be attached or removed from the wall sockets by their plugs without affecting the operation of Polynet. Alternatively, where increased flexibility is

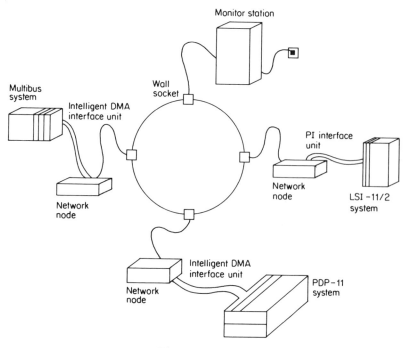

Fig. 12. Polynet.

necessary, 'daisy chaining' is also possible. This is achieved by the provision of an XLR plug and socket on each Polynet unit.

The network node has been so designed to support 2 bytes of user data either in a 38 or 40 bit circulating slot[26] and is attached directly to the network medium. A single 50 way ribbon cable connects the interface unit of the attached device to the node. Logica provide two kinds of Polynet interfaces: DMA and interrupt. The former provides point-to-point connection between attached devices at a data rate of 1 Mbps [44]. The latter provides a lower data rate of 100–300 kbps.

Costs for Polynet components are approximately £830 for a network node, £2800 for a monitor station, £390 for a LSI-11 interrupt interface, and £3500 for a PDP-11 DMA interface.

A restricted form of multicast or broadcast addressing is also included in addition to point-to-point addressing [45]. This is achieved when destination address 255 is used in the minipackets, but all nodes can only receive this minipacket as long as they are in a receptive state, i.e. not busy.

The manufacturers claim that future expansion of the programming interface to 8 data bytes per slot is possible without any modification to properly written software. The product has also supported voice and it is claimed that the available bandwidth is capable of allowing 30 simultaneous calls. Furthermore, it is asserted that the advantages of the Cambridge Ring include its guaranteed bandwidth and rate of delivery, ease of fault location and installation, and a far greater maximum length of ring cable [46].

6.1.1.4 TransRing 2000

TransRing 2000 (Scientific & Electronic Enterprises Ltd (SEEL) (UK)) [47] is SEEL's version of the Cambridge Ring and uses two twisted pairs for cabling and possesses a raw data rate of 10 Mbps.

Among the interfaces available are an Interface Interrupt Unibus, an Interrupt Q-bus, and a S-100 bus. A DMA Unibus interface and a DMA Q-bus interface are under development. A Z80A based terminal concentrator has just been released and is capable of supplying RS232C channels for 10 terminals [48].

SEEL claim that the TransRing data protocol facilitates the addition of a new processor to the LAN. Communication with all other processors attached to the ring is possible as this only requires a hardware and software interface between the new host and the ring.

The main modules for the system, i.e. the monitor station, repeater, and access logic, cost between £450 and £500 [49]. Current versions of TransRing are based on Eurocard-sized circuit boards designed by SEEL using MSI chips and there are plans to use a Ferranti ULA two chip when it becomes available.

Apart from the systems installed at SEEL's offices and the Edinburgh Regional Computing Centre, Hatfield Polytechnic and a group of southern universities have also set up their own TransRings.

6.1.1.5 Planet

Essentially, Planet (Racal Milgo Ltd (UK)) [50] is a 10 Mbps 'circulating slot' Cambridge Ring, but with the incorporation of some modifications. For instance, the minipacket is 42 bits in length where there are 16 bits of data and one 16 bit destination address contained. Compare this to other Cambridge Ring minipackets where both 8 bit source and destination addresses are included. Thus, Planet is capable of accommodating over 65000 addresses which could possibly be used on several interconnected rings. Furthermore, Planet assumes the form of a double ring of coaxial cable and does not use twisted pairs of wires like other Cambridge Ring products.

The components of the product include cable access points (CAPs), terminal access points (TAPs), and an administrator station. These correspond approximately to repeaters, stations, and the monitor station on other Cambridge Ring products. The CAPs are passive units and connect directly to the cable. The TAPs, which are microprocessor based, interface user devices and connect to the CAPs. They also possess the resident software which is responsible for packet transmission and reception over the network. The ring provides for standard V.24 connections for devices transmitting synchronously at up to 19.2 kbps, but no special interfaces to specific types of processors will be supplied.

The administrator station is functionally more complex than the monitor station on the more standard Cambridge Ring implementations. Included in the administrator station on Planet is a name server which would be provided by a functionally separate device on other Cambridge Rings. In simple terms, the function of the name server is to establish a call between two nodes by checking that the destination node exists and determining the location of the node. Thus, if the name server should malfunction then internode communication would not be possible. This necessitates the provision of a back-up server and in terms of the system implementation this presents no real problem but such duplication would usually result in increased cost.

Higher-level protocols to provide file transfer, transport service, and gateways for access to public packet networks are possible future offerings, but there is little information concerning the software available for the product.

Costs of the components comprising Planet are not readily available, but a starter pack for attaching six devices costs approximately £5000. The administrator station is the most expensive component and in a typical implementation of about 40 attached devices the approximate cost is £400 per attachment [51].

Racal claim that Planet is capable of 'repairing itself' and that it is more reliable than any other LAN product on the market [52]. When a failure is detected the administrator station automatically reconfigures the ring. For instance, if the coaxial cable[27] of Planet is severed, the station awaiting the message informs the network administrator. The latter retransmits the message in the opposite direction, in so doing reporting the cable break or terminal failure within one second. Compare this with the original Cambridge Ring which is inherently less reliable because every station needs to be active for the system to function. The implementation of Planet based on twin fibre optic rings may be a possible development.

6.1.2 Other ring products

6.1.2.1 SILK

The System for Integrated Local Communications (SILK) (Hasler (GB) Ltd) (Fig. 13) is a coaxial cable based LAN which handles packetized voice in addition to data traffic [53]. The bit transfer rate is 16.896 Mbps and the effective data rate approximates to 10 Mbps depending on the type of traffic [54,55].

Each loop may accommodate a maximum of 150 access equipments, e.g. local blocks (LBLs), at up to 100 m apart, to each of which it is possible to connect seven user devices. Hence, 1050 (7 x 150) devices in all may constitute a SILK system. The LBLs and the main blocks (MBLs) are responsible for traffic transmission and reception. SILK employs hardwiring to maximize the speed of the LAN whenever possible. However, other SILK equipment is microprocessor based whenever software control is deemed appropriate.

The media access protocol employed is register insertion and this is performed by the LBLs. All user equipments send their packets whenever they have them ready, enabling the loop to handle many packets at once. The packets are addressed to the desired destination, where they are subsequently removed from the loop and reassembled as an exact copy of the data originally transmitted. As the packet flow is unidirectional, the packet stream passing any one point on the loop implies that all other packets in the stream will pass that point in travelling from their source to their destination. Consequently, traffic on the loop varies from point to point as user information only traverses the arc between the origin and the destination.[28]

Hasler (GB) Ltd sells SILK as a LAN product only and does not concern itself with the aspects of software development or the nature of the attached hardware. An LBL costs approximately £3800 and a digital telephone approximately £1400 per line.

SILK is not susceptible to a single point failure disabling the system as a 'braiding system' is employed. Here, a continuous loop may be maintained as secondary and tertiary cable paths allow specific loop equipments or sections to be bypassed after failure at some point (Fig. 14).

The quality of transmission on SILK is also continually monitored by the regular flow of test packets around the loop. Advance warning of any deterioration and the initiation of braidswitching downstream is thus possible. Hasler claim the network is applicable for integrating data and speech in an office environment. An electronic mail system has also been implemented on SILK.

58

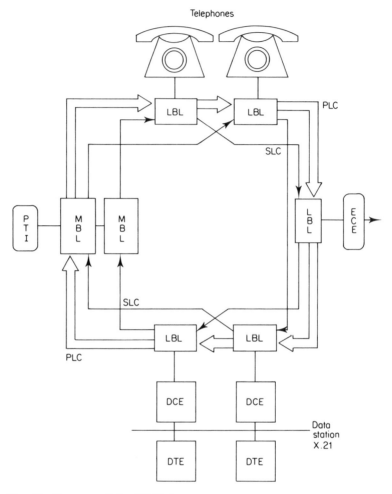

Fig. 13. Concept of the SILK loop: PLC, primary loop sections; SLC, secondary loop sections; PTI, portable test instrument; MBL, main block (duplicated); LBLs, (up to 150) local blocks; TCCs, terminal connection circuits (seven per LBL); data stations, X.21 interface; telephones, digital from PCM; ECE, connection equipment to external service; DCE, data circuit equipment; DTE, data terminal equipment.

6.1.2.2 Xinet/Xibus

This ring-based system (Xionics Ltd (UK)) [23,56] (Fig. 15) contains three principal elements: Xinet, the Xibus master node, and multifunction workstations.

Xinet is a ring-based LAN operating at approximately 1 Megabyte per second. It comprises 'intelligent sockets' interconnected by multicore cable. These devices are called communications adaptors and are able to contain the

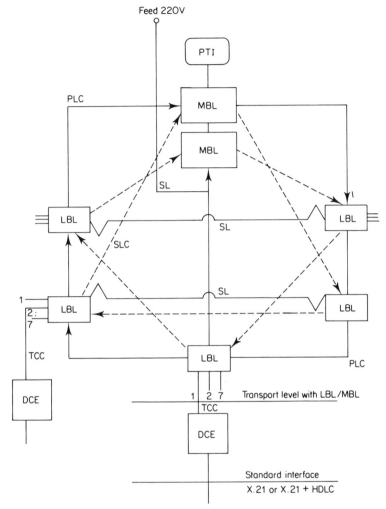

Fig. 14. The SILK 'braiding' structure: LBL, local block; MBL, main block; DCE, data transmission (carrier) unit; PLC, primary ring circuit; SLC, secondary ring circuit; SL, feeder; TCC, stub; HDLC, high-level data link control procedure; PTI, portable test instrument.

extensive software routines which are necessary for various network protocol levels. Each 'intelligent socket' possesses a packet of its own and therefore transmission does not involve the sockets competing for a limited number of slots.

The second constituent of the system is the Xibus master node. This is a multiple microprocesor resource combined with high-capacity Winchester technology disk drives and performs three main functions: first, to facilitate the sharing of a database; secondly, to present a location index for any data, resource or user forming part of the architecture; thirdly, to supervise the

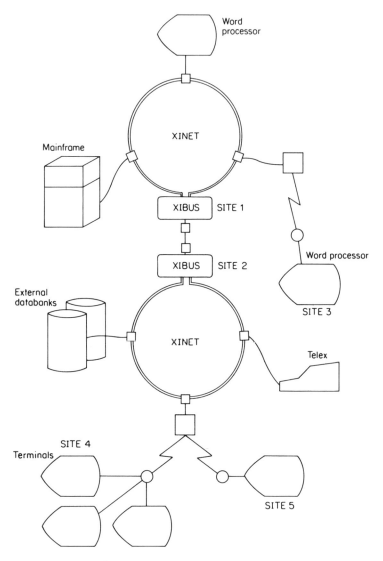

Fig. 15. A multiple-site Xibus system.

network by providing the database administrator with facilities to collect statistics and interrogate or alter configuration details.

The third system component is the multifunction workstation which is connected to an 'intelligent socket'. This allows users access to information sources and processing resources within the system.

The Xibus and the multifunction workstation cost £40000 and £2500 respectively. A communications adaptor, which essentially acts as a cluster controller, is available for around £3500.

The storage, retrieval, and processing of information is achieved by Xibus downloading the necessary software routings to the Z80 microprocessor based workstations. Programming languages available include Cobol and Basic.

The product has been designed for fully resilient operation and every functional module within Xibus is at least duplicated. This includes Xinet and the 'intelligent sockets'; duplicated rings operate in parallel in the former and socket logic is duplicated in the latter.

Xibus/Xinet does not restrict the type of data used and the architecture may be used for conventional computer records and transactions, textual documents, messages, and digitized speech.[29]

6.1.2.3 DOMAIN

This LAN product (Apollo Computer (UK) Ltd, Apollo Computer Inc. (USA)) [58] is claimed to be the first Distributed Operating Multi-Access Interactive Network (DOMAIN) and represents an alternative to dedicated time-sharing minicomputers. DOMAIN is a coaxial cable based ring and operates at 12 Mbps. The maximum permissible distance between nodes is 1000 m. Media access is achieved by a node capturing a token and only then may transmission proceed. When this is complete, the node passes on the token. At any instant only one token must be on the ring.

On the network, node-to-node interaction is maximized by the omission of superfluous buffering of messages. Thus, direct message exchange is possible between two communicating processes. Additionally, data transmission through a block multiplexer channel permits DMA devices to access the memory bandwidth between the two communicating machines.[30]

One of the principal design objectives of DOMAIN was the provision of a dedicated cpu for each individual user node. These nodes are personal computers based around twin Motorola 68000 microprocessors with an initial 512 kbytes of memory and with the capability to support 3.5 Mbytes of error correcting memory.

A virtual address space of 16 Mbytes in a UNIX-like environment is provided for each user. Furthermore, multiple processes generated by users no longer occur in a sequential manner but in a concurrent mode. Pascal and Fortran '77 compilers are currently supplied facilitating the conversion of existing programs.

Apollo claim that DOMAIN is appropriate for applications where there exists a high computational and high interactive requirement, and that the concept of a dedicated computer for each user enables the provision of a better service than the conventional time-sharing system.

6.1.2.4 ODR-1

This fibre optic based ring (Syscon Ltd (UK)) [167] consists of one controller and up to 15 slaves and utilizes a time division multiplexing technique with a self-clocking, self-synchronizing code developed by Syscon.

This code is based on a pulsewidth modulation technique where the width of a pulse indicates whether a bit is a data bit or is being used for synchronization purposes. The ring was also given RS232C compatibility and the slave units are designed as 'data communication equipment' (DCE) allowing them to interface directly to terminals. The controller, designed as 'data terminal equipment' (DTE), interfaces directly to computer serial input/output ports making the resulting link RS232C transparent.

Syscon break down the fibre optic system into three components: the fibre optic cable, the connectors, and the electronic interface.

The fibre optic cable is a low-cost plastic version which is capable of offering a 24 m link at 10 MHz. Increasing the length to 40 m is possible but the bandwidth has to be reduced. Connectors to fibre optic cable have always presented some problems. In this system, low-cost electrical jack plugs are used to make a demountable electrical connection to the medium. The makers regard that this electrical connector is more cost-effective than an optical connector. The electronic system for transmission and reception is not significantly different for fibre optic systems than for a wired system, when the data rates are reasonably low. The receiver is usually greater in capacity and one of the basic objectives was to have low power requirements and hence CMOS technology has been used. This does, however, limit encoding/decoding rates and provides a maximum system clock rate of approximately 5 MHz.

As the system is an active ring, all units must function for the ring to function.[31] In the event of slave failure, data transmission may only extend as far as the preceding slave and data received from the slave downstream of the failure. In cases where system requirements make failure intolerable, redundancy must be integrated into the system to ensure continuous operation. Consequently ODR-2, which is a dual-channel full duplex system (capable of surviving single station failure), is now offered.

ODR-1 is offered as a package (£5950) with one controller (£595) and each slave (£385). Each 25 m fibre optic link costs £43.75 [59].

Syscon have recognized that ODR-1 could be made more sophisticated, where possible enhancements include the data rate[32] and number of slaves supported, station separation, and optional interface specifications.

The current system bandwidth is adequate to support voice (16 kHz) and this would be provided as a special interface option. With these enhancements, Syscon regard their product as being suitable to support applications such as word processing and electronic mail in the office environment. Here, the controller would become an intelligent switch and the slaves would be connected to peripherals such as storage devices, printers, and VDUs.

6.1.2.5 Clearway

Clearway (Real Time Developments Ltd (UK)) [61] is a ring-based LAN product that interconnects user devices with standard RS232C asynchronous interfaces, over a maximum distance of 800 m.

There is not a great deal of information concerning this relatively new product, but the manufacturers explain that network access is analogous to register insertion, which is performed by junction boxes.

These junction boxes interface user devices to the ring and contain buffer storage for up to 'one and a half thousand characters', allowing the different baud rates of the communicating devices at each end of the connection to be accommodated. Each junction box collects a maximum of 33 characters and inserts a destination address and a checksum at the front and end of the packet respectively. The packet is then transmitted along the coaxial cable and forwarded by each subsequent junction incurring a two-character delay until it reaches its destination. The transmission rate is approximately 35 kbaud, which the makers claim is approximately equal to 3000 characters per second. The destination checks the packet and acknowledges its receipt. A stop-and-wait protocol is used, where each packet that is received is acknowledged to ensure that all packets are received in the correct order.

In theory a maximum of 99 units may be addressed as the 8 bit address is interpreted as two digits, i.e. 2 times 4 bits, but in practice the manufacturers recommend a limit of 50 units. Furthermore, each unit is informed whether it can establish connection directly with a destination or whether it must proceed via a third unit. The system is aimed for small configurations of around 12 VDUs each operating at 9.6 kbaud, but not requiring continuous data.

The cost of the Clearway components are low. Each node costing approximately £100 is inexpensive in comparison with other LAN products, but it is also very much simpler and possesses a relatively low data rate.

The system allows two alternative forms of wiring. One method is by establishing a series of junction boxes to which devices can be attached as required and the other method is by merely daisy chaining each of the nodes together, where a new node can be inserted merely by disconnecting and attaching the new junction box.

6.1.2.6 Multilink

This LAN (Hawker Siddeley Dynamics Engineering Ltd (UK)) is configured as a ring and connects up to 125 identical Multilink station units using a single twisted pair of wires at a data rate of 250 kbps. The manufacturers claim that the ring can possess a total length of 400 km although it is recommended that two stations should not be separated by more than 1 km.

The Multilink station units are Z80A microprocessor based and capable of effecting any necessary actions, e.g. code conversion. Each station unit is individually powered and furnishes an RS232C interface to a host at data rates (up to 19.2 kbps) which are completely independent of each station and this enables communications between processors and terminals to be supported.

The attached host unit could be a computer, an intelligent or dumb terminal or a peripheral unit. A number of microcomputers (Apple II, Newbury Newbrain, Zilog MCZ-2, and a Transam Triton) have been attached performing call establishment and data transfer routines [62]. Each host can have up to

30 channels (virtual circuits) and can receive data from a number of transmitting hosts without the receiving station carrying out any action. Up to 12 simultaneous two-way transmissions can take place at 19.2 kbaud without overloading the system. If messages are not acknowledged then they are retransmitted. The cost of each network interface is in the region of £300.

The Multilink LAN is unaffected if stations are switched on and off. Furthermore, it is possible to remove or insert stations physically without losing any data providing the ring is re-established within 10 seconds.

The data rate of 250 kbps is modest in comparison to some of the other LAN products, but the vendors consider this to be sufficient to support a large number of applications for links between processors and terminals. For instance, there are development plans for the inclusion of a library of routines to be implemented on a range of microcomputers. Other developments also include the implementation of a file store on a microcomputer with a hard disk and a high-speed parallel interface to the station units. Further, a software package will also be introduced to support an on-line sales order system with simultaneous invoice and packing document production.

6.1.2.7 Pronet

Pronet (Proteon Associates Inc. (USA)) [63] is a ring-based LAN product in which media access is achieved by the circulation of a control character, i.e. token passing. The addressing scheme employed can support up to 255 stations which transmit data on the ring up at 10 Mbps.

The hardware of the Pronet primarily consists of two circuit boards. One circuit board is the host interface and the other is a control card which is responsible for access to the network. The total cost of the two circuit boards is approximately $3200.

Pronet also includes driver software, but the operating system of the host still needs to be interfaced and integrated with the ring software.

The product is directed at users of DEC Unibus and Q-bus based machines, like the PDP-11 and the LSI-11. Also available are host interface circuit boards for the VAX machines running the RSX-11 and RSTS-11 operating systems.

Although the system is based on twisted pairs of wires for distances 'up to several thousand feet', coaxial cable, fibre optic, and microwave can be employed over greater distances. Network interconnection to other Pronet rings can also be achieved by gateways.

In this product, the user is responsible for adding the extra software needed to interface the operating system of the host to the ring and this may prove to be an undesirable feature. In defence, Proteon Associates assert that this causes only a minimal disruption and upheaval of the host and that the six Pronet implementations have only taken a few hours to install.

6.2 Non-Ring Products

The reader is referred to Tables 9 and 10.

TABLE 9
Non-Ring Products.

	Vendor(s)	Media access/ packet size	Data rate	Medium	Number of stations	Range	Interfaces	Comments
6.2.1 Single vendor supported LANs								
6.2.1.1 Cluster/ One	Zynar Ltd/ Nestar Systems	CSMA–CD	0.25 Mbps	16 wire ribbon (multicore)	65	300 m	Apple IIs, Apple IIIs only	Features include hard disk server, electronic mail facilities. Distributed financial planning system also available
6.2.1.2 HiNet	Extel/ Modata Ltd/ Digital Microsystems Inc.	TDM (SDLC)	0.5 Mbps	two twisted pairs	32	300 m	DSC-3s, DSC-4s	CP/M operating system. Network management software available
6.2.1.3 Omninet	Keen Computers Ltd Corvus Systems	CSMA	1 Mbps	twisted pair	64	1200 m	Originally Apple IIs only, Onyx C-800, DEC, LSI-11, Apple IIIs, S-100 bus	Datagram service offered—virtual circuit considered too expensive. Corvus Winchester disks are be installed on system. Omninet contains no collision detect circuitry. Positive acknowledgement protocol employed
6.2.1.4 Z-Net	Zilog (UK) Ltd/Thame Systems Ltd/ Zilog Inc.	CSMA–CD	0.8 Mbps	coaxial cable	255	2000 m	MCZ-2s only	Shared data station provides 10–40 Mbyte store

Table 9 (*contd.*)

6.2.2 *Multivendor supported LANs*

	Vendor	Access	Speed	Medium	Number	Distance	Interface/products	Notes
6.2.2.1 Econet	Acorn Computers Ltd	CSMA–CD	0.21 kbps	two twisted pairs	255	1000 m	Acorn Atom and other microcomputers, e.g. Acorn Proton	Aimed at educational institutions with computer aided learning software
6.2.2.2 Ethernet	Digital Equipment Corporation, Xerox Corp., Intel. Corp.	CSMA–CD	10 Mbps	coaxial cable	1024	~2700 m	DMA controllers are available for Unibus and LSI-11 bus, cpus	1st bit of 48 bit address indicates whether broadcasting or not. Of the 2^{47} addresses possible multicasting can be achieved by addressing a defined subset of device population. Xerox range of products including Star can interface to Ethernet
6.2.2.3 Hyperbus	Tesdata Ltd/ Network Systems Corporation	CSMA–CD	6.312 Mbps	coaxial cable	128 BIUs (max of 4 equipment interfaces per BIU)	700 m	B100/200—RS232C, B300—IBM 3270, B400—DMA (2 Mbps) B700/900—interconnect 2 Hyper buses	3 levels of network access priority: background, normal, alert. -hierarchical addressing scheme utilized. Hyperbus–Hyperbus interconnection provided pins. Hyperbus–Hyperchannel
6.2.2.4 Net/One	Thame Systems Ltd/ Ungermann–Bass Inc.	CSMA–CD	4 Mbps	coaxial cable	250 attachable systems	1200 m	NIU1—RS232C (non-prog.) NIU2—programmable	Software may be developed through network development station. Network Administrative Station—control + monitoring facility. Broadband version of Net/One to be released in future

TABLE 10
Non-Ring Products.

	Vendor(s)	Media access/ packet size	Data rate	Medium	Number of stations	Range	Interfaces	Comments
6.2.3 *Broadband systems*								
6.2.3.1 LocalNet	NTL/Sytek Inc.	CSMA–CD	System 20 $=120 \times 128$ kbps System 40 $=5 \times 2$ Mbps	coaxial cable	24000 (120 × 200) at 9.6 kbps	50 km	RS232C, DEC VAX + PDP-11, IBM mainframe	Bridge to Ethernet to be offered in 1983. IBM mainframe channel interface offered which emulates an IBM 3274 terminal cluster controller. IBM 3270 terminal access, voice packets and teleconferencing also supported—Gateways to Tymnet and Telenet available
6.2.3.2 WangNet	Wang (UK) Ltd/Wang Labs Inc.	CSMA–CD	12 Mbps (Wang Band)	'dual' coaxial cable	'65000 devices'	unspecified	RS232C, RS449 Wang Equipment	WangNet to serve user needs of data, voice and video transmission. Interconnect band for Wang and non-Wang devices in switched mode. Dataswitch polling device controls gateway modems
6.2.3.3 Videodata	Interactive Systems Inc./ 3M Corp.	TDM (Autopoll)	1.2 kbps– 96 kbps	coaxial cable	> 2000 attached systems	~10 km	RS232C	Security, time, and attendance monitor voice and video as optional applications. Also energy management systems

Table 10 (contd.)

6.2.3.4 BIS	Philips Data Systems	token passing	4 Mbps	coaxial cable	1024 Philips devices (4 stations can be connected to same node)	unspecified	RS232C (V.24), Philips computers	This product is due for release in 1983. Multimode communications (audio, video, data)
6.2.4 *High-speed LANs*								
6.2.4.1 HYPER-Channel	Tesdata Ltd/ Network Systems Corporation	CSMA–CD with priorities	50 Mbps per trunk	4 coaxial trunks	64 stations per trunk	300 m	CDC, IBM, Univac, Cray, DEC, Honeywell, DG, Tandem	~$45000 per interface. Installations include University of London Computer Centre
6.2.4.2 LCN	CDL/CDC	rotating priority access protocol	50 Mbps per trunk	4 coaxial trunks	25 stations per trunk	metres NADs 95 4 610 13 305 22 158 26 76 28	IBM 360, 370, 303X, DEC PDP-11, Unibus, CDC-6000, Cyber 170s, Cyber 200s	Each LCN needs a CDC Cyber. ~$43000 per interface. Software for file transfer between mainframes available
6.2.4.3 Ubits	Amecon Division, Litton Industries	CSMA	160 Mbps 45 Mbps (point-to-point)	19 twisted pairs (multicore)	127 logical hosts or terminals per NMU	unspecified (point-to-point) links possible	unspecified	Supports data, voice, facsimile, and video. Datagram and virtual circuit services provided. Attempts to conform to OSI reference model
6.2.4.4 IDX-3000	M/A-COM Linkabit Corp.	TDM (primary switch to 16 remote controllers)	393 Mbps	twisted pairs	3C72 peripherals, terminals and computers	1800 m	Interfaces with up to 128 MX24 multiplexers, others not specified	16 remote controllers connected to primary switch. Future enhancements to include voice, cryptography, packet-switch, protocol conversion

6.2.1 Single vendor supported LANs

6.2.1.1 Cluster/One

Cluster/One (Zynar Ltd (UK), Nestar Systems (USA)) [64,65] employs CSMA-CD and is a bus-based system using flat 16 wire ribbon cable supporting a data transmission rate of 0.24 Mbps (240 kbps). This LAN product is single vendor in the respect that, although up to 65 stations may be interconnected, these are solely Apple II or Apple III personal computers.

Network topology is not restricted, as bus, star or tree configurations, with the maximum of 65 stations acting as either users or servers, can be interconnected over a distance of 300 m. The distributed control of CSMA-CD allows stations to access the network. This is implemented by a layered set of protocols.

Level 0 is the physical network access. Here media access, collision detection, and address recognition are performed by hardware.

Level 1 is packet transmission, effected by ROM based firmware resident in the network interface card.

Level 2 is message transmission allowing multiple packets to be consolidated for interpretation as a single message. This is also performed by ROM based firmware resident in the interface card.

Level 3 is the 'process communication level', where the message is interpreted by software in the communicating stations.

Software supported by the Apple II and Apple III microcomputers include the operating systems DOS and CP/M and the languages Basic, UCSD-Pascal, Fortran, Assembler, and Cobol. The multiuser nature of the network necessitates the provision of a sophisticated file server software. The network facilitates multiple file servers where each file server is capable of accommodating up to 66 Mbytes of Winchester hard disk storage. This is, in essence, a fully featured back-end storage network providing a common file storage system.

Some approximate costs for Cluster/One are known. An Apple II microcomputer with dual double-sided 8 inch diskette drives and the network interface card costs in the region of £4500. The network interface card itself costs £350. The cost for 300 m of cable ranges between £1800 and £3000 depending on the quality of the cable used. The Winchester hard disk of 66 Mbytes would cost approximately £9500. Cluster/One runs a local area viewdata system, as well as electronic mail, teleconferencing, distributed financial planning, and word processing applications. Zynar have also developed a number of gateways to allow access to external networks and services. Among the features of these gateways are the ability to communicate with remote IBM and ICL mainframe and minicomputers, network-to-network file transfer, and access to Prestel.

Zynar chose to base their product on Apple IIs because of their popularity. It was considered that this factor together with the quantity of accessories available for these microcomputers would make the production of a LAN product easier and cheaper. Accordingly, the LAN is directed at small companies which would probably correspond to 20–40 stations. However, a number of large organizations have installed Cluster/One systems, e.g. the Central Computer and Telecommunications Authority (CCTA), the National Computing Centre (NCC), and Citibank, and Zynar have claimed 150 installations, 30 in the UK [66].

6.2.1.2 HiNet

HiNet (Extel (UK), Digital Microsystems (USA)) [13,67,170] (Fig. 16) is a single vendor supported LAN product in that it interconnects Digital Microsystems DSC-3 and DSC-4 microcomputers only, over distances up to 300 m. Access to the network is not distributed, but is achieved by a network master controller polling up to 32 slave units allowing transmission at a data rate of 0.5 Mbps.

Essentially, the network master controller behaves like a sophisticated I/O processor. SDLC is provided and thus a multidropped configuration is allowed where stations incorporate an RS422 interface to the cable. Expensive resources may be shared as they can be attached to the network master controller and this station must then be responsible for the use of such resources, e.g. disk storage and printers.

Each HiNet station could vary in complexity, ranging from a VDU user station (with Z80A microprocessor and 64k RAM) to a fully implemented station possessing its own local memory and printers, but either a DSC-3 or a DSC-4 microcomputer can be designated as network master controller. In cases where the network is sufficiently small, the network master controller can also function as a user workstation.

HiNet provides a virtual CP/M environment and thus a variety of CP/M compatible languages, utilities, and application packages can be employed, e.g. Basic, PL/1, Fortran, Cobol, and Pascal. HiNet provides two types of network management software: HiNet-1 and HiNet-2. It is claimed that the HiNet-1 network management software enhances the CP/M operating system by managing the networking and data communication aspects of the system in a user transparent manner and, where different users require access to the same files, file protect protocols are also available. HiNet-2 network management software provides the networking and data management of HiNet-1, but uses CP/M version 2, making application programs developed under the operating system accessible to the user. The Oasis operating system is available as optional software.

Some costs for HiNet are known. A DSC-3 microcomputer with 1 Mbyte of disk storage costs approximately £3530 and a DSC-4 multiuser computer with 1 Mbyte of floppy disk storage costs approximately £4400. A DSC-4 with 28

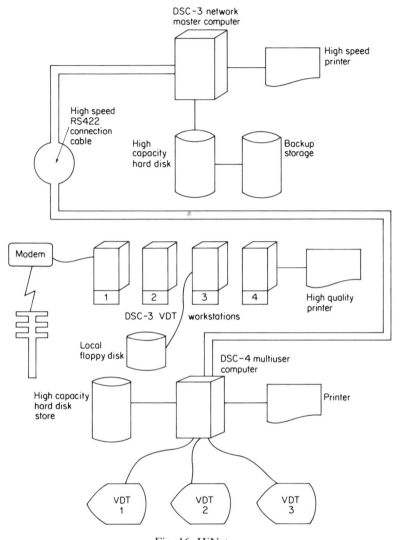

Fig. 16. HiNet.

Mbyte Winchester disk storage costs approximately £8400, and a Winchester disk as an add-on unit alone costs approximately £4500. HiNet-1 and HiNet-2 system software for DSC-3/4 costs £180 and £300 respectively and the cost of 300 m of cable necessary for the product would be in the region of £270.

The networking capabilities of HiNet can be added to any existing stand-alone DSC-3 computers. The addition of further workstations, to satisfy growing requirements, is achieved by their simple attachment to the RS422 network cable without any noticeable effect on the processing capability provided for the existing users.

72

In the UK, British Telecom has ordered seven HiNet systems for various applications, including holding information on private circuits and to store records of all orders. Midland Bank International and Credit Factoring International have also purchased HiNet systems. The former intends to use the product for software development for foreign exchange dealings and the latter to provide processing for user-generated applications.

6.2.1.3 Omninet

Omninet (Keen Computers Ltd (UK), Corvus Systems (USA)) [68,69] (Fig. 17) is a LAN product which allows up to 64 microcomputers to be interconnected over distances up to 1200 m.

The system employs CSMA as the access protocol which is implemented by circuitry in the network interface for each node, allowing a data transmission rate of 1 Mbps. These network interfaces are referred to by the makers of Omninet as 'transporters', because it is claimed that they implement the first four layers of the ISO OSI reference model, i.e. the physical, data link, network, and transport layers. These transporters contain the necessary processors and software to implement the functions of the network interface, and essentially there are nine integrated circuits which together interface a user device directly to the serial network.[33]

The vendors claim that there are two levels of carrier sensing used in the system and implemented in the transporter. At the first level, the network interface detects that there is no activity on the carrier for 15 microseconds and then informs the software in the host that transmission may commence. The software then instructs the interface logic control to start a transmission but, because a considerable period of time has elapsed since the carrier was first sensed, a second level of carrier sensing is initiated in high-speed logic. If there is activity on the carrier, then the transfer is aborted, otherwise transmission proceeds. It is thus claimed that collision detection is not necessary and this would only add to the complexity and expense of the system.

Every correctly received message is positively acknowledged on Omninet and if the acknowledgement has not arrived within 15 to 20 microseconds, the message is retransmitted. The receiving station, however, does not sense the carrier before sending the acknowledgement, as all other stations will have sensed activity on the carrier and still be waiting to transmit. The theory is that all acknowledgements will be sent and never lost through collisions.

The manufacturers claim that a micro virtual circuit service is provided at the transport layer instead of datagrams or virtual circuits. Note that in the ISO model these services are provided at the network layer and not the transport layer. Datagrams and virtual circuits were rejected because the former was considered inadequate for microcomputers and the latter too expensive. It is claimed that the so-called micro virtual circuit reaches a compromise because state information regarding the establishment of the circuit is only maintained for microseconds, but the service guarantees that a

73

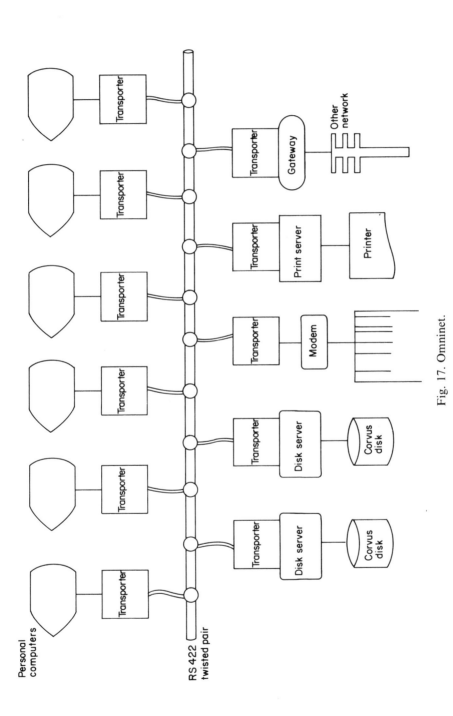

Fig. 17. Omninet.

message transmitted will be delivered correctly or, if not, that the source will be informed if the message has not been delivered.

In combination with the Corvus Constellation software, any microcomputer on the LAN can share 5–80 Mbytes of data, access a common database, and share the use of printers and graphics peripherals. Omninet effects the sharing of common storage by the use of a server, which contains a transporter, and an interface to a Corvus Winchester disk system.

Omninet has been classified as single vendor supported LAN product because it was originally intended for Apple II microcomputers. However, network interfaces for the Onyx C-8000 and the DEC LSI-11 have recently emerged and future releases are to include an interface for the Apple III, TRS-80, and S-100 bus microcomputers.

Some costs for Omninet are as follows. Transporters for an Apple II, a DEC LSI-11, and an Onyx C-8000 cost £350, £500, and £450 respectively. The Omninet disk server costs £700; 5, 10, and 18 Mbytes of hard disk cost £2300, £3650, and £4680 respectively.

6.2.1.4   Z-Net

Z-Net (Zilog (UK) Ltd, Zilog Inc. (USA)) [70–73] (Fig. 18) is a baseband CSMA-CD LAN product that can accommodate up to 255 systems over a distance of 1200 m.

A typical Z-Net is composed of three types of stations linked via a coaxial

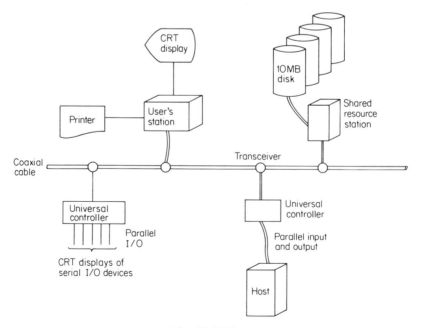

Fig. 18. Z-Net.

cable. The first type of station is the user station which generates or receives data. The second type, the shared resource station, allows the sharing of disk drivers or printers. The universal controller, which is the third type, handles dissimilar host-to-host communications. A microprocessor board and memory board form the heart of all three types of station. The microprocessor board contains a Z80A cpu, an RS232C interface, a parallel interface, and a Z-Net interface; the memory board, 6 kbytes of ROM and 64 kbytes of RAM. In the universal controller station, the Z80A and memory boards provide one serial interface and one parallel interface to connect devices to the LAN. The network interface circuit on the Z80A board permits each station to be linked to Z-Net without the need for central control.

Z-Net uses Zilog's MCZ software. This software is divided into three main layers. The first layer, the multitasking kernel, is the nucleus of the system and is the minimal piece of software needed to control the cpu resources. When priorities are equal, the kernel uses a round-robin method of scheduling. Each station on the network has a set of network protocols, which represents the second layer of software, and essentially Z-Net is a combination of hardware and this software that enables the exchange of information. These network protocols have two main layers, the 'data link layer' and the 'network control layer' which provide a 'reliable datagram service'. The top layer of the system software is a concurrent programming system called RIO/CP, which provides all the mechanisms to communicate with remote devices. Several languages are available from Zilog to run on its MCZ-2 systems; these include Cobol, PLZ/SYS, and Z80 Assembler.

More recently Z-Net II has been announced [74]. This package has been designed to allow the connection of multiple System 8000 users. Z-Net II itself is composed of three parts: Z-Net local area network, the System 8000 interface board,[34] and the higher-level communications protocols. The latter are an extended version of UNET,[35] which has been designed to provide a totally media-independent network communications for UNIX based machines.

The approximate cost of the Z-Net II package is $9000 for a licence fee and $6000 per system which includes the System 8000 network interface board, transceiver, and cables.

Z-Net, it is claimed, makes possible inter-office electronic mail with Z-Net itself running the intermachine and task synchronization provided by the kernel. Within the office automation context, Z-Net can provide communication facilities, common storage, and other shared resources.

6.2.2 *Multivendor supported LANS*

6.2.2.1 *Econet*

Econet (Acorn Computers Ltd (UK)) [75–77] is a low-cost baseband LAN product which employs CSMA-CD as the access protocol over a medium of two twisted pairs of wires. Econet uses an 8 bit address which allows up to 255 stations to be interconnected over distances up to 1 km and at a data transfer rate of 210 kbaud.

The hardware consists of the Econet interface and the station. The interface, or Econet Eurocard as it is called, fits into the Atom microcomputer station. The product was originally designed for Acorn Atom microcomputers but the makers claim that other types can be accommodated. Unfortunately, they do not actually specify which other types. Other hardware supported on Econet include a file station and a printer station. The former presents a shared disk facility and runs a 'file server' program. The latter runs a 'print server' program which will present files to the printer if it is available, or store the files on disk if the printer is not available. Both stations are Acorn systems.

Accordingly, the software for the product includes: the Econet interface software, the file server software, and the print server software. The Econet interface software, which is contained in a 4k EPROM, possesses the driver circuitry that connects the Atom microcomputer directly to the network. Furthermore, the Atom is able to generate the network clock and the maximum clock rate quoted for the system is 210 kHz. However, the effective rate, i.e. the rate at which a station can read data from a disk, is much lower than this. It takes 16 ms to read 256 bytes from a disk, and a further 6 ms for network transfer to occur. Thus, the total time is 22 ms resulting in an effective transfer rate of approximately 1 kbaud. There are other transfer overheads that have been ignored and these could lower the effective rate drastically. These include reading the directory from disk, disk latency, and waiting for the network to become available.[36]

The Econet software also includes the Network Operating System (NOS) and the low-level primitives which are called by the NOS. The NOS controls user commands from stations and the low-level primitives which can be called from user programs to implement special protocols.

The software associated with the other two hardware components, i.e. the file server program and the printer software, are designed to run on Acorn Atoms. The former controls disk space and provides a shared filing system for all users and the latter provides printing for one file at a time and maintains a queue of other files requiring printing.

The costs associated with Econet are low. An Econet interface costs less than £50 and the Acorn Atom microcomputer costs approximately £300. This perhaps justifies the makers claim that each station would cost less than a standard VDU terminal.

Acorn explain that the real motive for the design of this product was to enable Atom microcomputers and/or other systems to communicate and to share peripherals such as disks and printers. This modest system was developed for schools and colleges in particular, but it is claimed that the product is appropriate for office and business applications.

The ability to interconnect a number of Econets is allowed through gateways and among the other features of the product is the ability to handle the transmission of digital signals, such as speech. The manufacturers claim this LAN is able to cope with the two-way communication of digital speech and the one-way transmission of higher-quality signals, but there is no elaboration of these techniques.

6.2.2.2 Ethernet

The Ethernet (Digital Equipment Corporation, Intel Corporation, and Xerox Corporation) [3,4,11,14,29–31] is probably the most widely publicized of all the LAN products and, as outlined in Chapter 5, employs CSMA-CD as the media access protocol over a coaxial cable.

An individual Ethernet consists of a 500 m cable segment to which no more than 100 stations can be attached and where intercommunication takes place at a data rate of 10 Mbps. Repeaters can allow up to five of these 500 m segments to be interconnected where the nodes at the extreme ends of the Ethernet system cannot be separated by more than 2.7 km. This extended version of the Ethernet can allow up to 1024 stations to be attached.

The hardware components of the Ethernet consist of the coaxial cable transmission medium, a tap which connects the transceiver to the medium, a cable consisting of four twisted pairs of wires which interconnect the transceiver and the controller up to a maximum length of 50 m. The components which are really responsible for transmission are the transceiver and the controller. The former is responsible for carrier sensing, collision detection, and the transmission and reception of encoded data. The latter encapsulates and decapsulates the data, i.e. constructs and breaks down data packets, and is responsible for initiating or deferring transmission.

The Ethernet specifies a minimum packet size of 64 bytes and maximum packet size of 1518 bytes. This does not include the 8 byte preamble which allows all listening stations to prepare for the reception of packets. A minimum packet size of 64 bytes is determined by the maximum round-trip propagation time on the Ethernet system of a maximum length of approximately 2.7 km, at a data rate of 10 Mbps. If packets were any smaller and collision garbled the packet, the collision detect circuitry would not associate this with the transmitted packet. Thus, higher-level protocols would have to incorporate a method for realizing that the packet received was not the same as that transmitted and then call for retransmission.

Among the user device hardware offered for the Ethernet are workstations (Xerox 860 and 8010 Star), terminal servers, file servers (Xerox 8031), and printer servers (Xerox 8044).

The 48 bit address employed by the Ethernet can theoretically accommodate 2^{47} user devices. The first bit indicates whether the destination address on the packet is to a single device or a subset of the device population. Thus, Ethernet allows broadcasting and multicasting.

There is not much definitive information concerning Ethernet component costs at present, although companies which manufacture their own Ethernets under licence will allow some appreciation of the costs involved. For example, 3COM Ethernet products are priced approximately as follows: a transceiver costs £380, a coaxial cable terminator £20, a Unibus Controller £2150, a Q-bus controller £1800, and 15 m of coaxial cable £190 [78]. The following approximate costs are derived from Sension Scientific Ltd (UK). One transceiver £360, a coaxial cable terminator £12, a terminal interface controller £795, and a quad channel terminal interface controller £985 [79].

Information regarding software for Ethernet is currently lacking, but releases in 1983 and 1984 are expected. Xerox offer Courier, a transaction oriented remote procedure call protocol at the network layer for the higher layer protocols to build on. Such a protocol is useful, for example, in remote calls to a name server and receiving the results back [80].

DEC have integrated Ethernet into the Digital Network Architecture and the DECnet products [172], and higher-level functions such as network management, error recovery, and internetworking are now provided. The network management layer allows planning operation and maintenance of the network, in this case the Ethernet, through such aids as a cable fault detection and location and faulty node isolation.

Clearly there is a lot of information concerning the technical details of the Ethernet but little operational experience, particularly in the UK, where only a few such systems have actually been installed.

6.2.2.3   Hyperbus

Although Hyperbus (Network Systems Corporation (USA)) [81] is a coaxial cable baseband system operating at 6.312 Mbps and employing CSMA-CD, it is currently incompatible with Ethernet and presents an alternative architecture. Whereas the latter employs a unique 48 bit address, the Hyperbus address has two parts. The first byte and second byte of the address correspond to the BIU address and to the BIU port address respectively [82].

User devices are connected to the coaxial cable bus of a maximum length of 720 m via microprocessor based (dual 6809) bus interface units (BIUs). The system can accommodate up to 128 BIUs which vary in complexity according to the nature of the user equipment to be interfaced to the bus and which the vendors categorize according to four application groups.

The first group of BIUs (called the B100/B200 series) cost approximately $4000 each and interface RS232C terminal equipment and host communication ports via the Hyperbus. This BIU group resemble modems providing equipment and data protocol independence with full duplex operation at data rates from 110 bps to 19.2 kbps. In this group, a minicomputer multiplexer is also provided and this necessitates a special software driver be resident in the host computer, but this BIU can create 32 virtual RS232C ports on a pair of minicomputer DMA ports.

The B300 series form the second application group of BIUs and interface IBM 3270 equipment and controllers to Hyperbus. These BIUs permit single multidrop wiring of terminals, dial-in switching between the terminals and the controllers, and high-performance operation between terminals and controllers.

The third BIU group, DMA interfaces capable of data rates up to 2 Mbps, is provided by the B400 series. In this group individual B400 BIUs can maintain up to 64 virtual circuits for minicomputers communicating directly over the Hyperbus system.

The fourth and final group of BIUs concern link applications. The B700 is a gateway connecting a Hyperbus and a Hyperchannel. The B800 directly connects two Hyperbuses and the B900 connects two Hyperbuses via a standard communications facility.

Network Systems claim that the four groups of BIUs outlined above allow a hierarchical bus structure to be implemented. At the lowest level, a local bus interconnects user equipment. At the next level up, the local buses may themselves be interconnected either directly via a gateway device or via some communications media, e.g. fibre optics, resulting in the hierarchical structure.

Maintenance and network administration of the Hyperbus is also possible and provided by the Bus Service Centre. Its tasks include journalling of BIU information packets, security and special user self-testing routines (for bus ports and attached equipment) and assistance in dialling or verification of connections.

6.2.2.4 *Net/One*

Net/One (Thame Systems Ltd (UK), Ungermann-Bass (USA)) [83–85] (Fig. 19) is a 50 ohm coaxial cable bus based system which is compatible with Ethernet and has the ability to link a wide variety of manufacturers' equipment.[37] Net/One interfaces are completely passive and thus the network remains unaffected in the event of a node malfunction. Although the limit of Net/One is approximately 1200 m, further segments may be added via repeaters, allowing the connection of 'thousands of devices'. Gateways to other Net/Ones are also available.

Net/One hardware comprises passive transceivers and network interface units (NIUs). The latter are programmable allowing flexibility in protocol matching. A network development system (NDS) and a network administration station (NAS) may be added which enable the writing of software and the monitoring of the network respectively. These four types of components, e.g. transceivers, NIUs, a NDS, and a NAS, are the basic units of the network. The NIU handles packet processing, circuit connection, and error detection and can have connected to it multiple terminals or CPUs with RS232 or parallel ports. The more advanced NIUs possess the processing power required for application programs.

Data transmission through the LAN can occur in two different, user-selectable modes: datagram and virtual circuit. The former involves the one-

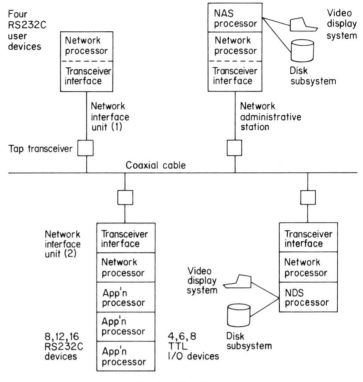

Fig. 19. Net/One.

way transmission of a packet. In the latter, the network appears as a full duplex, non-switched dedicated line. When the virtual circuit connection is set up, the network then becomes completely user transparent. Even a terminal with limited intelligence can be used because the NIU itself provides the Net/One intelligence. There are two complementary aspects to Net/One's ability to reconcile incompatible protocols. First, peripherals and processors on the network can be selected on the basis of performance rather than compatibility. Secondly, this allows potentially heterogeneous hardware at one location to be knitted together.

Ungermann-Bass designed Net/One to be compatible with Ethernet as the latter was regarded to be one of two networking standards likely to be adopted.[38] Note, however, that Ungermann-Bass are now offering a broadband LAN [86].

6.2.3 Broadband systems

Broadband networks allow several logically distinct networks to function on different frequency division multiplexed (FDM) channels. Such LANs are thus capable of sharing a cable with closed circuit television and other video services.

6.2.3.1 LocalNet

LocalNet (NTL (UK), Sytek (USA)) [87–90] utilizes coaxial cable as the physical communications medium. The vendors claim that the provision of high bandwidth (300–400 MHz) and multidrop capability goes some way to meeting growing data communication requirements.

The architecture of the system is structured on a layered set of services: the transmission layer, the network layer, and the user device interface layer. The transmission layer offers two types of channel: System 40 and System 20. The former is a 2 Mbps channel capable of interconnecting a small number of processor based systems via 'host interfaces'[39]. The latter can accommodate between 100 and 150 asynchronous terminals on each of its 120 channels (128 kbps). Media access is achieved using CSMA-CD.[40]

The network layer is implemented in each LocalNet packet communications unit. A so-called 'Tbox' performs all necessary media access, network intelligence, and user interface functions, and forms the basis for System 20.

The user interface layer is connected to the Tbox by an RS232C interface. This supports serial asynchronous data communication at selectable data rates to 9600 baud and optionally at 19.2 kbaud. Two levels of virtual control operations are provided to the user. The first level allows initialization of individual units, e.g. setting logical channel numbers, unit addresses, data rates. The second level is a subset of the first and allows the set-up, interruption, and termination of virtual circuits.

The vendors have recognized the desirability of certain enhancements. These include the capability for increased network interconnection, user device interfaces, security and privacy as upgradable features of the system.

6.2.3.2 WangNet

WangNet (Wang (UK) Ltd, Wang Laboratories Inc. (USA)) [91,92] is a twin coaxial cable based broadband LAN which has an available bandwidth of 340 MHz (10–350 MHz). On this system, attached devices transmit signals on one channel (of the forward cable) which with other channels constitute a band. The signals are received by stations on the same frequency channel as the original transmission but on the second cable and there is no shift in frequency like some other broadband products.[41] This is because the transmit and receiver circuitry are effectively attached to two different parts of the cable: transmit circuitry on the forward cable, receiver circuitry on the reverse cable.

The product can be configured to possess a branching tree topology and the main coaxial trunk doubles back on itself to form the dual coaxial cable system. This therefore allows the cable system to be divided into a transmit cable and a receive cable.

The 340 MHz of bandwidth is divided up into three separate bands, each of which is intended for a different purpose, but note that a large portion of the available bandwidth remains unused. These three bands are referred to by Wang as the Interconnect Band, the Utility Band and the Wang Band. The Interconnect Band (10–82 MHz) can in fact be divided into two types of channels—dedicated and switched channels. The dedicated channels, which occupy the frequency range of 10–22 MHz, can be further subdivided into thirty-two 9.6 kbps channels and sixteen 64 kbps channels and provide multipoint and non-switched point-to-point communications for any vendor equipment. User devices can be attached to these dedicated channels via fixed frequency modems and as the Interconnect Band is protocol-independent any communications protocol can be implemented.

There are also 256 9.6 kbps switched channels which occupy the frequency range 48–82 MHz in the Interconnect Band, permitting a maximum of 512 RS232 compatible devices to be interconnected. Circuit switched and point-to-point communication between devices occurs via frequency agile modems and a unit called DataSwitch, which controls access to one machine by another.

DataSwitch assigns one of the 256 9.6 kbps channels to two communicating devices in the following manner. When a device connected to this part of the Interconnect Band wishes to transmit to another attached device, the frequency agile modem, to which the device is connected, issues a request dialling the destination automatically or manually. The DataSwitch determines the availability of the destination and, if available, informs both devices of the frequency channel they should use to communicate. As the Interconnect Band is protocol-independent, no protocol translation is provided. Communicating devices are thus assumed to use external translators on an individual basis or the same protocol, but the switched portion of this band is dependent upon the reliability of the DataSwitch. In the event of failure of the DataSwitch, communication using this bandwidth would not be possible, thus some form of back-up would be necessary.

The Utility Band occupies the frequency range of 174–216 MHz and makes up to seven 6 MHz channels available for video applications. Passive components are employed and are attached to the medium to link video equipment. Freeze frame and full motion video signals can use these channels allowing applications like teleconferencing, security, and monitoring systems to be implemented.

The frequency range 217–253 MHz is occupied by the Wang Band, a 12 Mbps channel which employs the distributed control of CSMA-CD for intersystem communication among Wang equipment only and allowing files, documents, and peripheral devices to be shared.

WangNet employs a 16 bit address and thus it is theoretically possible to accommodate over 65000 devices. In practice, however, this may be unrealizable. The devices connect to the WangNet coaxial cable via a cable interface unit (CIU). The CIU is a Z80 microprocessor based intelligent controller that assembles data into variable length packets and then transmits them at the appropriate frequency. The reverse process is performed for packet reception. Thus, the CIU performs FDM in addition to possessing the necessary circuitry for implementing CSMA-CD. End-to-end flow control and complete error recovery on all transmissions will be implemented on the Wang Band and higher-level functions such as virtual terminal protocols and file transfer protocols will also be included in the future.

Some approximate costs are known for WangNet. The products and associated costs for the Interconnect Band are as follows. The 64 kbps (RS449) modems and the 9.6 kbps (RS232) modems for the dedicated channels of the Interconnect Band cost $1200 and $850 respectively. The 9.6 kbps frequency agile modems necessary for the switched channels of the Interconnect Band cost approximately $1250 and the DataSwitch is approximately $12000. On the Wang Band, a CIU costs approximately $3800 but, as it can attach up to 10 devices, Wang claim the cost is shared, i.e. $380 per device.

Other features available on WangNet include an electronic mail system (MAILWAY) and gateways to external networks. Wang also plans to support the X.25 protocol and IBM's System Network Architecture (SNA).

6.2.3.3 *Videodata*

Videodata Broadband Communications System (3M United Kingdom PLC) [93] is a broadband coaxial cable based LAN in which data may be transmitted at 0.1 to 2.1 Mbps with low error rates (1×10^{-8}). This is achieved by a 2 Mbps serial asynchronous broadband radiofrequency (RF) modem (Model 5991)[42] in conjunction with a Data Remodulator (Model 450).[43] The RF modem uses frequency shift key (FSK) modulation and interfaces to the network by one or two (optional) RF sockets. This allows its utilization in a single or dual coaxial cable system.

The Data Remodulator or 'head end' is responsible for accepting messages from the input channel (5–108 MHz) of the network and retransmitting them on the output channel (170–300 MHz) to the receiving user devices. The bandwidth of 108–170 MHz is not utilized, except as a guard band. Broadband systems which divide the bandwidth in this manner are sometimes referred to as 'mid split'.

As its name implies, Videodata is designed for a fully loaded broadband CATV system where other channels are used for data, monitoring, and control systems. The aspect of monitoring and control makes the system applicable for security and energy management applications in building and several such systems have already been implemented.

Videodata uses time division multiplexing (TDM) as well as frequency division multiplexing (FDM) on the same cable. Thus, interfaces are available for dedicated FDM channels or TDM channels at particular frequencies. A polling mechanism called Autopoll uses two 800 kHz channels to achieve full duplex operation with terminals operating at up to 9600 bps. Autopoll's protocol can be employed by any minicomputer or mainframe computer attached to the 'head end' to control transmission from stations using the same channel. Autopoll is in fact implemented on each of the possible 35 independent 100 kbps TDM channels which individually may accommodate 248 terminals.

The makers of Videodata intend to release 5 Mbps and 10 Mbps modems as well as frequency agile modems which permit attached user devices to access more than one channel of the 100-plus channels that may be available.

A series of network products oriented towards IBM 3270 communications protocols has also been released. In this series a Model 6732 performs the role of an IBM 3274 Cluster Controller in communicating with up to 32 computer ports, while Models 6704 and 6708 will accommodate clusters up to 4 and 8 terminals respectively.

Some component costs of Videodata are known and are as follows. Model 5991, and the 5 Mbps and 10 Mbps modems will all cost approximately £300 and the Data Remodulator is priced around £1000. The IBM 3270 oriented equipment costs approximately £300 for a Model 6732 and approximately £2150 and £2300 for Model 6704 and Model 6708 terminal clusters respectively.

6.2.3.4 BIS

BIS (Broadband Intercommunication System) (Philips Business Systems) [94] is a broadband LAN based on coaxial cable where media access to two dedicated frequency channels is gained through token passing.[44]

Two types of data links are differentiated on BIS: point-to-point links between two predetermined stations over a dedicated frequency, and a multipoint channel, referred to as the Philips Intercommunication Pipe (PHIP). The former replaces a dedicated physical point-to-point connection between two stations by a dedicated, logical point-to-point connection. This is achieved by allocating a dedicated channel in the bandwidth to the two devices. In the latter, intercommunication at a data rate of 4 Mbps between 1024 Philips' computers and different equipment having standard V.24 (RS232) interfaces is possible. Two dedicated frequency channels are time-shared between stations connected to the PHIP and a pilot unit is required to synchronize data exchange.[45]

Unlike other broadband systems, access to the PHIP band is determined by a 'logical' token passing scheme. The sequence in which the stations transmit is determined at implementation time, and their transmissions in the lower half of the bandwidth are received by the 'head end', which broadcasts the message at a shifted frequency to all stations connected to the PHIP.

The intercommunciation unit of the stations themselves is in two parts, and implemented according to the ISO OSI reference model. The first part, the physical control layer, is located in a separate box which is called the multistation-interconnection unit (MSIU) and can be shared between four user devices. The MSIU performs modulation, demodulation, bit synchronization and presents a high-speed interface between the physical layer and the data link layer.

The second part, the data link and other upper layers, is contained in the station. The data link layer performs the PHIP access, i.e. token passing, and message preprocessing before communicating them to the software level by means of direct access to the computer's main memory (DMA). Other functions of this second part include error detection and recovery and global flow control.

At the time of going to press there were no cost figures available to the authors as the product had not been officially released. The product is expected to become commercially available in 1983.

Philips claim that BIS evolved from the need to meet their own requirements for factory automation and distributed office systems, by using mass produced technology and permitting data, voice, and video communications.

6.2.4 High-speed LANs

6.2.4.1 Hyperchannel

A Hyperchannel system (Tesdata (UK), Network Systems Corp. (USA)) [11,95–97] (Fig. 20) in reality comprises only two elements: a coaxial cable and the adaptors where the former provides a data highway between the latter.

Hyperchannel's adaptors are 100 Mbps buffered microprocessor based units which interface standard computing hardware to a Hyperchannel protocol implemented over a passive medium. The equipment and trunk interfaces directly access the buffers enabling both interfaces to operate at 50 Mbps. As each adaptor can support four trunks the maximum data rate of a full configuration is 200 Mbps (4 x 50 Mbps). The data rate and cable quality are determinants of trunk length, but at 50 Mbps using coaxial cable, 300 m is attainable.

In all, three types of adaptors are supplied: processor adaptors which interface a processor data channel to the trunks of Hyperchannel; device adaptors which interface a specific line of peripheral control units to the trunk by data channel emulation; link adaptors providing a gateway which interconnects two Hyperchannels.

Media access is achieved using CSMA. All adaptors contend for the use of the bus, but additionally a priority scheme exists to safeguard the data communications requirements of high-priority devices. The needs of these are satisfied before catering for the needs of lower-priority devices.[46] The priority scheme is implemented by enforcing a delay after each packet transmission which is proportional to the priority of the device, i.e. high- priority devices experience short delays while low-priority devices experience long delays.

Data and control information are transmitted on Hyperchannel in variable length figures of 23 bytes to 2 kbytes using a baseband phase modulation technique. The adaptors, which buffer data, communicate by an end-to-end protocol, and provide code conversion, can only accept frames addressed to them and then positively acknowledge their receipt. If the source does not receive a positive acknowledgement within 20 ms, retransmission takes place.

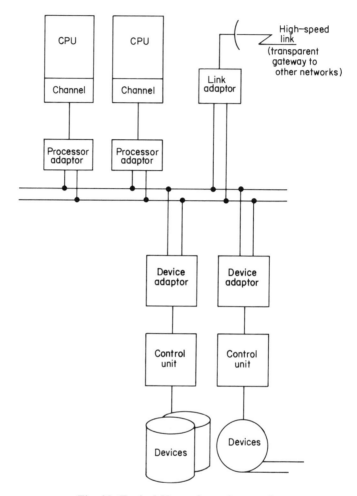

Fig. 20. Typical Hyperchannel network.

The network interface adaptors of the Hyperchannel are able to interconnect mainframe and minicomputers of many different manufacturers. The vendors claim that the adaptors on offer interface to over 80% of installed computing hardware. Some of the supported manufacturers are IBM, DEC, CDC, Honeywell, Cray, Burroughs, Tandem, and Data General. Extra software is, however, necessary to enable the applications and operating systems of these different systems to be interlinked, so that file transfer and the driving of peripheral devices may take place.

The cost of these network interface adaptors is not inexpensive and is in the region of £27000 to £28000. The customized software required to allow different computer systems to intercommunicate costs from £5000 to £15000.

A mass storage system is also available for Hyperchannel. Called Massnet, this software furnishes a virtual shared storage system and network management system for population of processors interconnected by Hyperchannel. The network manager module of the software allows application programs coded in Cobol, Fortran, PL/I or IBM Assembler to share the resources under the control of other processors [98].

6.2.4.2 Loosely Coupled Network

Loosely Coupled Network (LCN) (CDL (UK), CDC (USA)) [99,100] is a high-speed LAN product allowing mainframe computers to intercommunicate over a distance not greater than 900 m.

LCN employs network access nodes (NADs), where one NAD connects a node (one processor and one peripheral device) to the network. The LCN configuration allows multiple trunks and multiple NADs, thus eliminating the possibility of a single point failure disabling the entire system. Individual NADs can be attached simultaneously to as many as four different trunks, where each trunk can accommodate a maximum of 27 different NADs. This results in a total network capacity of 108 different units.

The role of the NAD itself includes handling message flows, allocating buffer memory, logging errors, and recovery and code conversion amongst various other system functions.

Data are transmitted in user-defined blocks of 512–4096 bytes. This occurs, as the vendors describe, in a synchronous burst mode, where NAD access is determined by a 'self-synchronizing, rotating priority mechanism'. This is essentially a decentralized time division multiplexing technique, where the media access protocol can be described as token passing.

LCN's host-to-host software, Remote Host Facility (RHF), enables multiple mainframes to interface with each other. RHF defines permanent file transfer, the transfer of job and output files, the interaction of different applications, tape staging, interactive and operator display, all within the guidelines of the ISO OSI-7 layered model at levels 5, 6, and 7. Although these layers have yet to be internationally formalized, the hope is that this will facilitate the accommodation of different mainframes and operating systems.

A NAD costs in the range $40 000—$50 000.

Akin to Hyperchannel, LCN is designed for use in a heterogeneous environment of different vendor machines, but unlike Hyperchannel, a CDC Cyber mainframe is required in every LCN. The claim made by CDC is that the complexities of contention are thus avoided (cf. Hyperchannel).

6.2.4.3 Ubits

Ubits (Universal bus information transfer system) (Amecon Division, Litton Industries (USA)) [101] is a recent LAN product that consists of one or more high-speed local networks. These local networks are interconnected at global interface units (GIUs) via serial point-to-point links at data rates of 45 Mbps, which may use fibre optic, microwave or satellite facilities.

On Ubits, devices are interconnected locally to a high-speed (160 Mbps) bus, which consists of multiple twisted pairs of wires forming a multicore cable. There are 16 data lines, a parity line, an activity indicator line, and a clockline on this cable.

Network management units (NMUs) are actually responsible for interfacing the devices to the cable and allowing stations to access the network via CSMA. Likewise, a GIU contends for the local bus using this same protocol, but there is no contention across the point-to-point links.

The NMU itself is microprocessor based and possesses a redundant CPU in case of failure. It is capable of supporting up to 127 logical hosts or terminals and is designed for a throughput of 10000 packets per second. It is possible to draw a distinction between the NMU's network-oriented and user-oriented functions. The former include PAD (packet assembly/disassembly), flow control and error control, and the latter are referred to as programmable interface modules (PIMs) and are application-dependent. A PIM interfaces to the network hardware via a shared memory on a common access bus.

Generalized network control functions, such as end-to-end flow control, error control, and a virtual circuit capability, are offered. The user interface (NMU) is conferred with considerable intelligence and provides transport and connectivity to a wide variety of devices and not to a specific vendor's equipment. Thus, the network can provide code, speed, and protocol conversion.

Although media access is decentralized on Ubits, one NMU (task director) performs two centralized management functions: network control and quality control. Its responsibilities include initialization of other NMUs, monitoring, and reconfiguration of the network.

Essentially, the GIUs on the Ubits system function as gateways and are programmed to receive only those packets that are specifically addressed to it. These packets are subsequently forwarded to those destinations across the point-to-point links. The GIUs perform no other processing except parallel to serial conversion and temporary data buffering.

At the time of going to press, no cost figures were available to the authors. Ubits resulted from a military command, control, and communications application where there is a need for an integrated system offering digitized voice, video, and data applications in a real-time environment.

6.2.4.4 IDX-3000

The IDX-3000 (Linkabit Corporation, M/A-COM Inc. (USA)) [102] is a high-speed digitally switched LAN which has recently been announced by the Linkabit Corporation.

The manufacturers claim that the system is distributed in terms of its architecture, but essentially it is comprised of 16 remote controllers which are connected to a central primary switch unit. Furthermore, the system is capable of interconnecting a total of 3072 peripherals and computers, where each remote controller can alone accommodate 192 such devices connected by full duplex twisted pair lines which can operate in a synchronous manner (at a data rate of 56 kbps) or asynchronous manner (at a data rate of 19.2 kbps).

This system architecture represents a centralized or hierarchical nature where media access is not distributed, but determined by the remote controllers and the primary switching unit. The total data rate claimed for the system is 393 Mbps and the primary central switch operates in a non-blocking manner, i.e. all data calls from the remote controllers are allowed to go through.

At the time of going to print no further information was available to the authors.

The product displays a very high aggregate data rate which is sufficient for switching voice, but the hierarchical structure distinguishes it from most other LAN products offered and also renders it susceptible to the problem of central reliablity and dependability. This product has been included to illustrate the wide variety of systems offered that are categorized as LANs.

Chapter 7
Other Considerations in LAN Evaluation

To some degree, LAN evaluation was considered in Part I of the book when topologies and control strategies were considered. This is true also when the features of the Ethernet and the Cambridge Ring were highlighted and some comparisons between the two technologies were drawn.

In this chapter, some additional factors will be considered. Essentially, these factors fall into two groups: technical and non-technical.

7.1 Other Technical Factors

7.1.1 Transmission media

Most LANs in use or being designed use bit serial transmission over either coaxial or twisted pair. The geographical restrictions encountered by LANs are those which come about when attempting to send high-speed digital information over such wire or cable.

7.1.1.1 Telephone twisted pair

This is relatively inexpensive but is prone to electrical interference from adjacent cores in the cable and external sources, e.g. fluorescent lighting and heavy electrical loads. At low data rates and when the current loop technique is employed, distances up to 1 km or so can easily be covered and cost-effectiveness maximized. If greater distances or higher data rates of up to 9600 bps are required, the cable system needs line driving equipment or more usually modems which conform to V.24 or RS232C standards. Current loop and V.24 usually demand that the LAN form a star configuration and thus additional terminals require additional points on the star itself. This problem is overcome by a number of manufacturers offering multidropping or multiplexing systems allowing more than one terminal to be connected to one pair of wires, but the terminal must possess sufficient intelligence to recognize the data intended for it and also transmit data to the common line when other terminals are inactive. Corruption of data must be prevented by relatively complex data checking procedures [103].

7.1.1.2 Screened multicore cable

This possesses a metallic screen which reduces the susceptibility of the cable to electrical interference and the intercore cable capacitance can be reduced to prevent intercore interference whilst simultaneously permitting greater data rates. The drawbacks with this type of cable are that it is far more expensive than twisted pair and yet still suffers from the same problems which occur with star networks. These problems are related to the use of multicore cable in the form of a data bus in which some cores carry data usually in a parallel form and others are used for addressing and strobing functions. This type of system is only designed for a given application and failure of one core makes fault location difficult [103].

7.1.1.3 Coaxial cable

This can be used where high-speed data signals are required over distances up to 1 km. This cable consists of a single central conductor surrounded by a concentric dielectric which in turn is surrounded by a metallic screen, minimizing electrical interference.

Coaxial cable permits data signalling in the broadband mode where many data signals are simultaneously carried, e.g. WangNet and LocalNet. Here each data signal is carried by a radio signal of a specific but different frequency confined to the coaxial cable so that the effects of electrical interference may be reduced. The benefits of broadband over baseband are clear, whereas baseband can only carry one data signal over the cable at any one time, broadband can simultaneously carry hundreds of signals [103].

Conventional flexible coaxial cable does, however, suffer from a number of disadvantages which prevent its use over long distances. Baseband utilization can reduce the effective distance of the cable to 300 m unless the shape of the data waveform is designed to prevent fast changes in voltage levels. The main drawbacks are that cable losses reduce the data signal to below an acceptable level and the screening is not 100% effective.

7.1.1.4 Fibre optics

Fibre optic transmission systems are currently attracting a good deal of attention and provide an extremely efficient method of data transmission on a point-to-point basis. Tapping into the fibre and extracting the signal, however, is most difficult and expensive. Until this feature becomes simple and inexpensive it is unlikely that this technology will become part of the LAN scene. The breakthrough could come through the development of multispectra high-speed light sources and the use of simple optical filters for the extraction of required wavelengths [104].

7.1.2 Hosts and their interfaces

LAN hardware is geared for high performance at low cost and the host interface generally provides all the transmission control and address recognition needed. The desire for the connection of low-cost minicomputer and microprocessor systems to LANs means that interfaces must be as inexpensive as possible. Eventually this could mean the LSI implementation of a host interface.

For the reasons cited above it is necessary to assess the interfaces available as they play a crucial role in the acceptance of LAN technology in general.

Simply, interfaces possess two parts: a *network oriented part* and a *host specific part*. The former performs those transmission control functions required for the network itself and the latter controls the data exchange between the attached host and the network oriented part of the interface [7].

Owing to the simple topologies and control strategies adopted by LANs a reduction in the complexity and the cost of the network oriented part of the interface is possible. However, the host oriented portion is a different matter. Microprocessor system interfaces tend to be the least complex because of their simple bus structures and the availability of LSI peripheral interface circuits. Larger-scale systems require more complex interfaces and minicomputer systems tend to need even more complex interfaces of the DMA type for high bandwidth peripheral devices.

The reduced complexity of the network oriented part of the LAN interface and the low cost of transmission medium shifts the cost of host attachment to a network from the network oriented portion to the host related costs.

The insertion of a front-end processor (FEP) has been one approach adopted by those not wishing to develop specialized hardware interfaces. The FEP approach however is less satisfactory for the attachment of a large-scale host to a LAN as the actual data rates available through standard interfaces mimicking RJE or interactive terminal ports are not particularly high. Effectively, the potential offered by the LAN is lost through front-ending. The development of specialized hardware and software to interface a large-scale host may initially be the most expensive route to follow but is likely to produce the best results as the data rates of a high-speed LAN and a large-scale host system are well matched.

The PDP-11 DMA interfaces are typical of the most specific part of a LAN minicomputer interface and for some microprocessor systems also. The latter are available as LSI chips but are generally half duplex interfaces requiring two for full duplex operation. The advantages of the full duplex nature of the interface are the initiation of a transmission operation whilst a receive operation is pending. The importance of this is that the receiver has no control over the time of the arrival of the message. Thus, if a host cannot perform a receive DMA transaction while the transmit operation is in progress, the message addressed to the host will be lost.

Modification of interfaces for various LAN types is also another issue. Here little attention to the host specific part of the interface is needed as the nature of data interchange with the host remains the same.

With the maturation of LAN and the accompanying standardization, the addition of LAN controllers alongside other LSI data communication chips will make high- performance LAN technology available at a reasonable cost.

In terms of the Ethernet, the controller functions, which include encoding/decoding, serial-to-parallel conversion, address recognition, error detection, and the basic CSMA-CD channel management, can be logically separated into transmitter and receiver functions. These functions are usually implemented as a combination of hardware, microcode, and software, but advances in LSI technology will mean that these functions will become available on a single chip.

Shoch *et al.* [33] assert that as many functions as possible should be transferred to the chip as long as this provides flexible system interfaces and flexible higher-level software. The exact allocation of the functions between the controller and the station is implementation-dependent.

The advantages of using programmable LSI circuits as serial data communications interfaces resides in the fact that the functional density of LSI circuits reduces the size, cost, and power of corresponding hardware while the programmable density allows the same part to be employed as a standard component throughout the system [105]. Programmability confers the benefit of adaptability. Alterations in baud rates, character lengths, error checking, transmission formats, and protocols are facilitated through the reconfiguration of mode and control registers.

Ultimately, this has a significant effect on redesign time and cost as well as the minimization of system obsolescence.

7.2   Other Non-Technical Factors

The brevity of this section is unavoidable because of the lack of concrete facts that can be offered owing to the almost total concentration by vendors and developers on the technical performance of LANs.

A number of factors are important in the implementation of a LAN, apart from the technical ones. In some ways they are more important to the potential implementer as he may lack the technical expertise to solve a problem which has developed in a LAN.

7.2.1   Maintenance

Maintenance of a LAN is of crucial importance, but there are some problems associated with this factor. The heterogeneity of vendor equipments that will undoubtedly accompany the proliferation of LANs may cause problems such as with whom the responsibility for maintenance lies. It could be the network vendor, the interface vendor or the attached host vendor. CDC with LCN guarantee the maintenance of all other vendor equipments attached to the network but this causes anxieties as to the proficiency of CDC maintenance contractors tending other manufacturers' equipment.

Another aspect of maintenance stems from the fact that many of these LANs are the result of systems established in academic institutions. The inevitable question that arises here is, 'Would the maintenance of the same LAN be possible to the same degree in a commercial environment?' The abundance of technical experts in an academic institution facilitates the diagnosis and the treatment of faults which may have developed in the LANs but do such counterparts exist in a commercial environment?

The situation where a cable may be severed causes maintenance problems, whether it is a ring or a bus network. The former allows the identification of a cable break between two repeaters but this could be up to 200 m. The latter causes a more vexing problem as the contention system relies on the reflection of its signal which obviously would not be possible if the cable was severed. The problem is exacerbated if the cable severance occurred in the ducts under a road. Clearly then there is a need for diagnostic equipment which is also portable and easy to use. The fact that LANs can be made to perform at very low error rates does not preclude the occurrence of faults at some time.

7.2.2 Security and integrity

Security and integrity of the LAN are other important factors. Yet many of the LANs considered mention no form of security or integrity at all. Xionics offers a duplication of hardware, software, and stored data. SILK allows the 'braiding' of transmission media which makes possible alternative routing, and Planet duplicates its lines of transmission and can detect errors at nodes within the duration of one packet cycle time. Duplication presumably implies duplication of costs as well, but in general it is a disturbing fact that security and back-up in the event of LAN failure appears not to be of prime importance to many LAN vendors.

7.2.3 Installation

Installation of LANs should be possible with the minimum of disruption to staff as well as the minimum of structural alteration to the building or site. These should not be ignored in the cost-benefit analysis of the possible implementation of a LAN. Also in the cost-benefit analysis the necessity of staff retraining should not be overlooked.

7.2.4 Extensibility

Extensibility of a LAN is a factor that should be given consideration, especially in the light of the stability of the environment in which the LAN is to be implemented. If the organization envisages greater staff and departmental mobility and thus their associated systems, then LAN configuration is a major factor. Also, the rate of growth of organizational computing means that modular growth of a LAN is significant. In this respect the passive nature of the contention system and the ability to tap into the cable is an advantage and allows the attachment of hosts and peripherals to proceed relatively easily. Furthermore, reconfiguration of the LAN may also be necessitated and this is more difficult to achieve with a ring which may require the attachment of a gateway owing to the active nature of the ring itself and its repeaters.

There are undoubtedly other non-technical factors that would influence a prospective LAN implementer but these would be very much a function of the environment in which the LAN would be established. The purpose of this section has been to focus the reader's attention to the inescapable fact that LANs should be considered not only in technical but alongside other non-technical terms as well. In the longer term, the latter may prove to be of more importance.

Chapter 8

Future Developments Affecting LANs

The recent technical history in networking is not dissimilar to other areas of computing: there have been dramatic advances in technology through stages of design and development, enhancement, followed by redesign. One perspective that could be adopted is that LANs are essentially a redesign of packet switching technology to make it cheaper, faster, and more generally useful. There are indications however that the two major failings of packet networks, viz. higher-level protocols and host interfaces, are being neglected—this time in the LAN context. This will be examined later in the chapter.

8.1 The 'Super-Intelligent' Terminal or the Management Workstation

It is difficult to estimate what the full impact of microelectronics on computer communications will be but it must be obvious that it will be highly significant. One such particular development could be that of the 'super-intelligent' terminal—a hybrid of an intelligent terminal and a minicomputer. It would retail for a few thousand dollars and permit a single user to have terminal access to a modest amount of local processing and storage as well as network access to general computer resources. A particular operation may be the performance of an inquiry/response task to a local database which in turn generates queries to remote databases. Simultaneously, remote users may be accessing the database at this 'super-intelligent' terminal and it has been suggested that LAN technology should be oriented to support this type of machine which will be capable of supporting and controlling several independent streams of data at the same time [10].

There appear to be two contrasting philosophies regarding the 'super-intelligent' terminal: the Computer Laboratory at the University of Cambridge approach and that of Xerox's Ethernet. The latter's philosophy is that of a 'computer in every office' approach to distributed processing and is demonstrable by the Xerox Star. The Cambridge Model Distributed System (CMDS) is an alternative to the Xerox approach and is flexible in an environment of heterogeneous machines and economical in terms of the hardware resources required to support a local user community. The CMDS services for organizing uncommitted machines encourage the implementation of distributed computations running on several machines. Thus, the most important aspect of the CMDS is its processor bank, an uncommitted group of minicomputers [22].

8.2 Baseband and Broadband Systems

The discussion about the relative merits of broadband over baseband systems—and vice versa—has been going on for some time. Of the LAN products discussed, few were of the broadband variety. This is because the cost of broadband technology is great in comparison to baseband technology.[47] In its simplest form, the argument or trade-off between the two is cost versus bandwidth/data rate. (The relationship between bandwidth and data rate is a positive one, i.e. the greater the bandwidth the greater the data rate, and is discussed more fully in Appendix D.) Basebands employ much lower bandwidths—usually no more than 50 MHz—and the bandwidth is taken up by transmitting one signal.

Bandwidth of broadband systems is usually far greater than that of basebands. It is often of the order of 300 MHz or more. For bidirectional use the system is usually split into two 150 MHz channels. To divide these channels further, to permit multiple uses, frequency division multiplexing (FDM), i.e. allocating different frequencies for different communication channels, or time division multiplexing (TDM), i.e. allocating different channels to use the medium at different times, is used. Alternatively, both strategies could be employed. Channels could be developed using FDM and then using TDM to form new channels within the existing ones, e.g. Videodata.

Most broadband systems available today use FDM (see WangNet) and have as their primary advantage the ability to handle video transmission. For use in video transmission, broadband systems usually have their available bandwidth broken up into a number of channels—often 6 to 10 MHz channels. Each of these channels has the potential for transmitting image, data, voice, and text. It must also be noted that the size of the channel, in MHz, is related to distance; the greater the distance, the greater the bandwidth has to be. There is also a need for guard bands between channels. Thus, the number of channels possible on a broadband system is related to what is being transmitted and over what distances. (See Appendix E to compare how broadband LANs utilize the total bandwidth differently.)

The aim of broadband systems is to provide a LAN with the capability of handling large numbers of devices over distances up to 10 miles and carrying data, image, and voice transmission [4,14]. Baseband systems are generally regarded as being insufficient for continuous video or voice applications and thus have a much more limited role. Yet, baseband systems are much less expensive and are available today. Broadbands are just now making their way into the marketplace, and those which have are very costly.

It has been reported that there are at least eleven US companies which are developing broadband LANs, including Wang, Bolt Beranek and Newman, DEC, and others [31]. It has even been suggested that IBM is working on a broadband system, but no official announcement has been made. Ungermann-Bass also plan to release a broadband product sometime in 1982 [17].

8.3 LAN-LAN and LAN-WAN Interconnection

The motivations for interconnecting local area networks to each other (LAN-LAN) and to wide area networks (LAN-WAN) have already been discussed. This is basically the inability to provide a local solution to user requirements in an economical manner.

Much effort is now being expended to interconnect LANs and many architectural and procedural questions require resolution before internetworking can be achieved on any reliable basis. These problems arise in relation to addressing, differing message formats, routing, and error control.

The principal aim of internetworking could be regarded as achieving the cooperation of remote computer systems [107] where the basic objective is to extend the features of a single network into an internet configuration [108].

At a less general level, LANs should be capable of supporting connectionless and connection type operations and where packet transportation between local or remote LANs is required, then the network layer of the OSI reference model is utilized to perform this interconnecting function.

Furthermore, the incorporation and implementation of one transport-network protocol set, to effect localized intra/internodal and remote internodal transport functions, has been regarded as a prime objective [109]. It is considered that this will facilitate the uniform construction of user nodes and hence result in greater standardization and increase the value to manufacturers and users alike.

If the interconnection of two networks is to be achieved, then one of the major design considerations would be to minimize the changes in hardware, software or protocols in both networks. Thus, a dilemma exists as intercommunication cannot occur unless the same protocols are used and yet the objective is to allow two machines using different protocols to communicate [3].

So what solutions are there to this problem? The basic problem with internetworking is either the modification of internal communication structure of the interconnected system or the insertion of a specialized device called a *gateway*. If the gateway solution is chosen then the system must know through which gateway the destination can be reached. The use of an internetwork protocol means that the system need not know, as the interconnected subnetworks manage the addressing schemes of all users autonomously.

The function of the gateway itself can be stated simply as packet conversion from one protocol to another. There are two different approaches as to how this conversion is to be implemented. The gateway could be responsible for directly converting the packet of one subnetwork into the packet of another and vice versa. Alternatively, the gateway could convert the packet into a standard internetwork packet. In the first case, the gateway is responsible for placing the packet of one subnetwork into another subnetwork. Consider, however, if three subnetworks are completely interconnected. Here the number of packet conversions that have to be performed is six. When four subnetworks are completely interconnected, the number of packet conversions that have to be performed by the gateways equals 12. The general case for n subnetworks which are completely interconnected means that $n(n-1)$ conversions will need to be performed.

The alternative approach, i.e. converting packets into a standard internetwork form, produces fewer conversions in circumstances where the number of interconnected subnetworks is in excess of three. For example, if two subnetworks are interconnected, then the number of packet conversions that the gateways will have to perform will equal four. First of all, the subnetwork packet will require conversion to the standard internetwork packet and then the subsequent reconversion from the internetwork packet to the other subnetwork. This accounts for two packet conversions and the reverse process accounts for the other two, giving a total of four. If the number of interconnected subnetworks is three, then there will be an extra conversion of the internetwork packet on the forward and on the reverse path giving a total of six. Employing a standard internetwork packet means that for the general case of n completely interconnected subnetworks, $2n$ conversions will occur.

In terms of the number of packet conversions that have to be performed, it is only advantageous to use the standard internetwork packet when the number of completely interconnected subnetworks is four or more, i.e. $2n$ results in eight conversions and $n(n-1)$ in 12 conversions.

In terms of flexibility, however, using the standard internetwork packet means that each gateway must perform two conversions whereas direct packet conversion into another subnetwork packet results in increasing gateway complexity with an increasing number of subnetworks.

In general, the type of service offered to the transport layer by the network layer impacts upon the design of the former. Thus the use of the internetwork protocol X.75 and the services it offers is very much related to the use of virtual circuit connections. Here, the essential feature is that the transport layer explicitly requests that the network layer establish a connection to a specific destination. This may be operationalized by setting up the internetwork connection by the concatenation of a series of gateway-to-gateway virtual circuits.

The datagram (connectionless) approach to internetworking is a complete contrast to the virtual circuit approach. Whereas the latter established a logical link prior to information frame exchange which is guaranteed to be sequential and error free, the former does not guarantee delivery, acknowledge frames nor provide any form of flow control or error recovery. In addition, the datagram approach does not require packets to traverse the same sequence of gateways. Here, each packet contains the complete source and destination address where the gateway performs the appropriate translation. X.75 is applicable to gateway-to-gateway lines and in effect specifies that concatenated virtual circuits require that all packets traverse the same gateway-to-gateway virtual circuits in sequence.

Thus, compatibility could be achieved either by protocol conversion (the performance of the appropriate transformation on messages as they pass through the gateway) or the adoption of WAN protocols by LANs. Caution must be exercised with the latter approach, in that LAN capabilities are not sacrificed for the ease of network interconnection [17]. Thus there are two constraints. As WANs are unable to provide all the functions that LANs can, and if LANs are designed to serve only the function of host connection to WANs, then the protocols of LANs may be designed to serve solely the communication requirements needed for WANs to the detriment of the other attributes that make LANs attractive. However, if LAN protocols are designed without generality, interconnection with other networks may prove extremely difficult or not cost-effective.

However, the use of gateways does present problems. For instance, even if the data link protocols are common to both subnetworks, no real modification may be necessary but an addressing problem may exist. This may require a new field in the header thus resulting in a major change. But if the subnetwork protocols are different, then even more problems will ensue.

The addresses may only have any real meaning within the boundaries of the LAN and thus some form of network layer addressing is required in order to perform gateway internetworking so that packets may traverse LANs.

If there are several gateways along one route then the gateways must implement at least layers 1 to 3 of the OSI reference model. If higher-level protocols (layers 4 to 7) of the subnetwork are inconsistent, then the gateway must be responsible for the higher-level protocol translation [110].

Matching the different speeds of LANs and WANs also requires resolution, as it is more probable that the former will have a higher data rate. If a host sends a large number of packets into the LAN with an ultimate destination to be reached through a WAN, then the packets transmitted will arrive at the gateway at a rate greater than that at which the gateway can forward them. Thus, the gateway needs a mechanism to prevent the exhaustion of the buffer space, but this problem is not peculiar to LAN-WAN interconnection as it occurs any time two networks of differing speeds are connected together. However, in this case the problems may be exacerbated because of the greater speeds encountered in LANs. It is possible that the gateway could attain quite a high level of complexity as additional features such as flow control may also be resident.

Other problems include which device should be responsible for the routing, i.e. the gateway or the source host, and who should maintain the gateway.

Elden [109] has suggested the need for a standardized approach to gateways. The adoption of X.25 and its incorporation into IEEE 802 as a gateway, which would possess a routing sublayer of network layer 3, has been proposed. At the start of the establishment of logical channel each internodal process-process session must be identified as intra-LAN and not inter-LAN and this can only be achieved by encoding some destination address field. Thus, at the link level, two station addresses are employed—one set for inter-LAN communication, the other for intra-LAN communication. This proliferation of protocols requires additional software development and ultimately extra cost. The problems of protocols, however, will be further considered in the next part of this chapter.

(Dallas [111] at the University of Kent has implemented an X.25 gateway to a packet switched WAN on a Cambridge Ring local area network. A DEC PDP-11 minicomputer was selected for use as the gateway and the RSX-11M operating system was chosen because of its suitability for a real-time environment.)

Thus, there are problems meeting the requirement for the connection of a distributed computer system to a national or even a worldwide network based on the use of leased lines or satellite links. Investigations into the linking of LANs to satellite services are already taking place in the USA with the cooperation of Ungermann-Bass and Comsat General [112]. In the UK the Science Research Council (SRC) have also proposed methods for satellite links [108]. The satellite characteristics considered in this scheme are those of the Stella experiment sponsored by the EEC; namely, the use of an Orbital Test Satellite (OTS) operating at a transmission speed of 1–2 Mbps with a 300 ms delay and requiring a 3 m diameter dish for reception.

On a more local level Clark *et al.* introduce a subnetwork concept which they consider occupies the middle ground between the monolithic, single-technology LAN and the internetworking environment as expounded above [7].

Here, the LAN is made up of a number of subnetworks of different technologies and transmission rates, but using identical software protocols, compatible packet sizes, and a single overall homogeneous address space. One single homogeneous address space means that one set of addresses is used for the whole of the LAN and is not solely applicable to an individual constituent subnetwork with its own address set.

The interconnection of these constituent subnetworks of varying technologies that make up the LAN is achieved by *bridges* which are midway in complexity between the multisegment repeaters, which are used on the Ethernet, and the gateways described above. The multisegment repeaters allow a number of individual Ethernets to be interconnected over a local area in a manner which prevents transmissions on one segment interfering with the transmissions on the other. This repeater will recognize destination addresses that do not belong to the segment from which the packet originated. Thus, it will selectively remove the packet and transmit it in another segment according to the same media access protocol, i.e. CSMA-CD. Similarly, a bridge repeats packets discriminately according to a 'filter function', i.e. the selective removal of packets addressed to other subnetworks, and speed matching may be performed as well.

However, bridges are more complex than the multisegment repeaters described above, because the speed and the media access protocol employed to access another subnetwork may not be the same as the subnetwork from which the packet was derived. Its complexity is not as considerable as a gateway, as the packet sizes, software protocols, and addresses require no conversion. The benefits afforded by this subnetworking concept are that a number of technologies and data rates can be utilized and this also confers an orderly method for accommodating any system growth. By decomposing a single LAN into a number of interconnected subnetworks, any enhancements or developments that are required may be introduced without impinging on the remainder of the LAN. Furthermore, some LAN technologies may be more appropriate for particular applications than others and thus the LAN can exploit the advantages that each technology can provide, yet overall still form an integrated network.

In order to perform these functions, a bridge will contain two network interfaces, a limited amount of packet buffer memory, and 'filter function'. The packet buffer will be necessary, as the receipt of the message from one subnetwork will require a subsequent retransmission determined by the control structure of the subnetwork to which the message will be forwarded. The key aspect that differentiates a gateway and a bridge is that no ordinary data packets are ever addressed to the bridge, whereas in internetworking a host about to transmit a packet must be aware of the fact that the destination address is on a different network. Bridges must determine whether or not a packet should be selected for retransmission, e.g. by a subnetwork field or a look-up table. Hence, a gateway will be responsible for inserting the destination address of the station according to the addressing scheme used on that particular subnetwork, whereas a bridge merely forwards that packet without any address conversion. Thus, subnetworking has relatively little impact on key characteristics of the network and addressing may be only slightly affected.

8.4 Protocols and Standards

McQuillan has ventured the following observations on communication networks [10]:

(1) the communication subnetwork has always been designed first by network people;
(2 higher-level network functions have always been designed later and by network people;
(3) the user's concerns have had lowest priority;
(4) widespread acceptance and use among the real user community has taken several years to achieve after network installation;

(5) some of the major costs and one of the reasons for the delayed acceptance in networks has been the delay in design and implementation of *higher-level protocols* and functions.

From these observations it is possible to discern that protocols and standards developments should play a major role in the acceptance of LANs. This section is essentially divided into two parts: protocols and LAN standards. In the protocol section, attention will be focused on the characteristics of LANs that impact on their protocols; the standards section will describe the current efforts to standardize LANs.

8.4.1 *Protocols for LANs*

As in WANs, LAN protocols can be divided into two basic levels—low-level and high-level protocols.

The function of low-level protocols is to transport groups of bits reliably through the network with the necessary timeliness. These protocols are not aware of the meaning of the transported bits and two LAN aspects influence the design of the protocols. First, the higher performance of LANs allows simplification of protocols and, secondly, low-level protocols must preserve the special capabilities of LANs, in order that higher-level protocols can also utilize these special capabilities [7,113].

Since LANs must support a wide range of hosts, the existence of extremely simple hosts leads to the need for simple, flexible, low-level protocols which can be implemented on small hosts whilst not reducing the performance of larger hosts. In WANs, complexity results from the attempt to utilize as much of the bandwidth as possible, whereas in LANs costs are concentrated in the host interfaces, the hosts themselves, and their software. Two factors allow the simplification of low-level protocols. As bandwidth is of no real concern in a LAN, there is no need to include protocol features to reduce the size of overhead bits sent with each message. The low transmission delay concomitant with the high data rates eliminates the requirement for buffer management, flow control, and network congestion control mechanisms. However, these characteristics cannot eliminate the disparity which may exist between two communicating hosts and consequently protocols still need to be designed with the necessary generality to surmount this problem.

The other aspect of LAN low-level protocols is the manner in which they are structured to capitalize on and provide to higher levels the unique capabilities of LANs. Conventional low-level protocols have provided a function test characterized as a bidirectional stream of bits between two communicating entities—a *virtual circuit*. Two other forms of communication which can easily be provided by LANs are *message exchange* (where the packets exchanged are not viewed in sequence but as isolated exchanges, i.e. datagrams) and *broadcast communication* (in which messages are sent not to one particular recipient but to a selected subset of potential recipients).

These alternative models of communication have not been implemented in WANs, because the major use of WANs has been for long-term, human initiated interactions with computers and not computer-computer interactions [7]. One problem that is handled in the context of a sequence of messages is the acknowledgement that the receiver has correctly received a message. If the messages are sequenced, then acknowledgement presents no difficulty but if they bear no relationship to each other, then each must be uniquely identified by the sender and acknowledged uniquely by the receiver, increasing the complexity and the overhead of acknowledgement. In the broadcast context, it is much more difficult to define an acknowledgement that can be supported by a low-level protocol.

What effect does this have on low-level protocol structures? From the discussion above, there should be two layers. The bottom layer should provide the basic function of delivering an addressed message to its destination, corresponding to the concept of a datagram network. The responsibility for detecting whether the message has been damaged in transit should also be assigned to this bottom layer but it should not be responsible for ensuring message delivery. Above this layer, a variety of protocols should be available, e.g. virtual circuit mechanism support, sending isolated messages, message exchange, and other models of communication.

The function of low-level protocols is really to support higher-level protocols and in the context of LANs the particular applications which are best suited to them.

A simple but important application of LANs is to solve the problems of an increasing workload by the deployment of another machine, in so doing dividing the applications amongst the machines. The communication problem to be solved is simple but critical—to allow an individual terminal to have access to both of the central machines. Thus, this access to common resources permits computing installations to grow economically. In fact, the LAN can be used to move computations from one machine to another in order to spread the computingload equally and the high speeds possible on LANs make this distribution of load much more practicable than do the bandwidths traditionally available in long haul networks.

If the computing power is not strongly centralized, a wide variety of new uses for the LAN arise. A completely distributed environment does not eliminate the need for an interconnecting network as users will still need to exchange information, e.g. computer mail, access to specialized resources, etc.[48]

Modification of higher-level protocols, to take advantage of the attributes of a LAN, is a problem of modifying the operating system of the host connected to the LAN, so that the services available through the network appear to be a naturally integrated part of the programming environment system and is not a problem of modifying the protocols themselves. One approach is to think in terms of a number of computers not necessarily of similar design, running under the same operating system. The operating system is so designed to present a user connected to one computer with a uniform and convenient way of accessing files or running jobs on other computers. Thus, it has been considered that what is needed is the concept of a network operating system among all of the devices, providing for distributed data processing and distributed databases [7,8].

8.4.2 Standards for LANs

There are a number of standards issues relating to LANs and these will be mentioned in this section. There seems little likelihood that any one standard will be adopted and at best there will be, in all probability, a few such standards.

In the UK, the Focus Committee which reports to the Department of Industry (DoI) has recognized the need for LAN standards [117]. However, it is interesting to note that this standards effort has included PABXs in the consideration of LANs. In addition to a discussion of the technologies and techniques used on the LANs, the report produces a functional classification in which there are four classes of LANs. The first class, called micronets, are essentially characterized by their low cost and the limited number of stations which they can accommodate. Non-integrated networks which represent the second class include broadband LANs and PABXs. The third group, integrated networks, also includes broadband systems, but with real-time voice capability, and high- speed baseband systems. The fourth and final class, videonets, includes those networks which possess the additional functionality of video transmission. Although the report is useful, it does not consider in great detail issues such as media access protocols which can be implemented on LANs and is very much dependent on the more comprehensive and intense standardization effort of the IEEE Project 802 in this respect.

In the US the IEEE, with its Project 802, is undoubtedly making the greatest attempt to standardize LANs and it is generally recognized that they are considering two alternative strategies. One standard, based on contention of channel capacity by attached devices (CSMA-CD), is unlikely to be ignored because of the Ethernet and the weight of its commercial support. The other standard is at present an unspecified token passing scheme and is less well developed but likely to have an impact in broadband networking, where data are transmitted on a modulated carrier frequency on a shared cable [118,119]. IBM's recent announcement that they have purchased the right to use a token passing patent held by O. Soderblom has thrown the whole issue of a token passing standard into confusion. It seems only IBM has known about this 15 year old patent and this has left Project 802 reeling [120].

Although the ISO OSI-7 [168] layered model is significant in LAN development, it is not without its problems and critics [121]. Bringing together the methods used in many different applications and by many systems suppliers would be quite a task and work would be needed on the upper levels of the OSI reference model. It is possible that the upper level functions (the application, presentation, and the session control layers) could be worked independently of lower level ones and could remain consistent across different types of lower levels. One of the key elements missing in most LAN discussions is the set of higher-level protocols which would be necessary to manage the flow of information amongst intelligent devices attached to the LAN. It is essential that these higher protocols be a part of a general communication architecture and should be based in an international standard if there is to be manufacturer support [10].

The Ethernet has attracted a great deal of manufacturers' support but initially there were substantial differences between the IEEE drafted functional requirements and the present Ethernct concept as proposed by Xerox, DEC, and Intel [169]. The IEEE local network standards committee wanted the standard to include a modem (the physical layer), and the interface (the data link layer) between the users' equipment and the modem. This interface would permit access to the network. The rationale behind this is that if this is done, then the user need only replace the modem to convert a signal transmission technology like coaxial cable into fibre optic, infrared or some combination. However, Ethernet is a coaxial network only and dependent upon a specific modulation technique. Problems also arise in the handshaking procedures and various error checks are used as insurance against signal loss. The IEEE standards committee regard Ethernet as using its own protocol rather than a standard such as HDLC and this makes it difficult to realize this safeguard. Error detection in Ethernet is handled by user software in as yet unspecified ways and this allows each device to be on its own, creating incompatibilities. (See Appendix F for a fuller treatment on the recommendations of Project 802 in relation to the ISO OSI-7 layered model.)

Thus, the work of the IEEE Project 802 has not been easy. Some critics claim that it is too early and with the present uncertainty, LAN standardization is impossible—especially in the light of 90% of the total standardization problem being at higher levels in the ISO OSI-7 layer architecture. Yet others disagree. Cotton [11] and McQuillan [10] do not regard LAN standardization as premature. Both consider the lack of effective standards across many different LAN systems as problematic and likely to impede the widespread adoption of this technology due both to incompatibilities among different components within LANs and to incompatibilities at the interfaces between devices and LANs, LANs and LANs, and LANs and WANs. Rapid acceptance of LANs will be achieved only if LANs offer attachments to terminals and equipment in use as opposed to a future standard for which there is no market. On the other hand, although the development of standards for WANs has been proceeding, it is still unclear to what extent these standards are applicable to LANs. It has been suggested that an inexpensive network interface is the most urgently needed standard for LANs.

8.5 Commercial Aspects of LAN Standards

LAN standards need the support of standard setting bodies and the commitment of manufacturers and user acceptance. The computer systems market possesses a long history of standardization through commercial dominance and thus the influence of the major manufacturers is crucial.

The promotion of Ethernet by Xerox, DEC, and Intel and its issue of Ethernet licences to over 200 companies including ICL, Olivetti, Hewlett Packard, Nixdorf, Ungermann-Bass, and Zilog will be significant in the contention of a LAN standard. Xerox's hope is that Ethernet will become the *de facto* standard of the industry—with or without the backing of the IEEE. And with the more licences Xerox sells, the closer is this goal to realization.

IBM's involvement in LANs has been unclear (see Appendix H), but at present it does offer a proprietary local network system as part of its 8100 distributed processing system. This local net uses two twisted pairs and possesses loop topology. An 8140 processor can be connected to a maximum of 19 local loops, but all devices on one loop must operate at the same speed. Loops may be up to two miles long at speeds up to 9600 bps or one mile at 38.4 kbps. Direct attachment of loops to an 8100 system processor without modems is possible or they can be attached through data links using modems at speeds up to 9600 bps [14].

IBM has expressed support within IEEE Project 802 for a token passing system being developed as the standard but this is interpreted as a political move intended to inhibit the *de facto* standardization of the Ethernet. IBM's goal, in this respect, is likely to be the integration of LANs in such a way as not to interfere with IBM's centralized philosophy. This would require a great deal of attention to gateways providing functions such as addressing, protocol management, and formatting. If maximum communication among the expected diversity of LANs is to be achieved, host-to-host protocols are required. Datagrams may be routed by a variety of communication modes like all packet switching data streams, and thus IBM's networking concept will use a dynamic programming algorithm to find the shortest available path for each internet message [122]. In the past few years, IBM has been committed to the philosophy of a computer as a central controller, a philosophy diametrically opposed to LANs. This is derived from SNA, which is a design framework within which IBM is directing future hardware and software developments with the aim of full communications compatibility among all IBM computer-based products. SNA at present is structured around the capabilities and constraints associated with long-distance communications networks, but it also shares several objectives in common with LAN design, e.g. full interconnection among all network devices and flexibility in arrangements for interconnection of such devices.

With the announcement of the Displaywriter and the IBM microcomputer, the merging of IBM's Office Products and General Systems Division, and the intention to interconnect different product ranges, some form of network product range is essential for IBM. IBM's recent X.25 commitment is an indication that IBM realizes that it needs to be flexible in its approach and hence a high-speed token passing LAN as an alternative to SDLC in SNA would come as no surprise.

And, as was mentioned earlier, IBM's purchase of the Soderblom patent for a reported $7 million is just one more indication of IBM's intention of introducing some form of token passing LAN. (The question which most people are asking is will IBM's LAN be baseband or broadband. The latest rumours are that IBM will introduce two LANs: one baseband which will be announced shortly, and one broadband which is probably a year away from announcement.)

Wang is a company which has achieved a significant commercial presence in the office automation area recently, and with WangNet it possesses a LAN product which is less concerned with the two alternative standards strategies proposed by IEEE due to its broadband technology. Wang's strategy appears to be that of offering a great degree of flexibility through its broadband LAN in the hope of achieving some degree of commercial dominance. This dominance is possible in that WangNet is one of the few LANs which allow the interconnection of video, data, and text devices.

In sum, the number of LANs available is growing at an astounding rate. In fact, there seems to be a new LAN product announced almost every week and a potential implementor of a LAN faces a daunting task in evaluating these various products. There are so many LANs vying for a place in the office systems marketplace that, whatever effects standardization have in the long term, the short term promises undoubted confusion. With the emergence of the new companies marketing LANs, any implementor of the system must be cautious of the reputation and stability of the company. Factors such as maintenance of the LAN and the equipment attached to it become crucial in addition to the technical merits of the LAN product itself.

In this respect, Cambridge Ring products have been at a disadvantage in comparison to the commercial support for Ethernet. However, in the UK support from the Joint Network Team along with Racal Milgo's new entry into the market with Planet may have a considerable commercial impact on potential purchasers of such systems [52,123].

8.6 Legal Aspects of LANs

Finally, a mention should be made regarding the legal developments which may affect LAN acceptance, e.g. the issue of whether organizations are at liberty to establish private data communications systems including the construction of private transmission facilities. In the US and the UK, it seems reasonably clear that where the facilities are owned and used by a single organization and where they are solely on the organization's site, the establishment of private transmission facilities will be permitted. However, transmission facilities which cross public roads, or are shared by different users or even offered for resale, pose numerous thorny issues which are at present mostly unresolved. These legal issues become even more complicated with the interconnection of LANs to both public and private WANs and all such issues will require address and deliberation before LANs can enjoy general use and acceptance [11].

Chapter 9

Some Organizational Implications of LANs

It is, of course, very difficult to predict what the organizational implications of LANs will be because LANs are really in their infancy. The effects of LANs on organizations will be related to: (a) what LAN is used; (b) what devices are attached to it; (c) what scope there is for expansion; (d) what provisions are made for security, back-up and recovery, integrity, etc.; (e) what the organizational philosophy is towards LANs, e.g. just a means to interconnect micros with word processors or to interconnect micros with mainframes and word processors, or to interconnect all sorts of devices with one another, and so on; (f) the organization's experience with computers and other forms of information technology; (g) the organization's information services plan; and (h) other organizational variables associated with both the internal and external environment. At present there are very few organizations using LANs[49] and thus there is little experience upon which to base any conclusions. Nevertheless, there appear to be two key organizational factors which would likely dictate the way a LAN affects a given organization. They are: (1) what the organization perceives the purpose of a LAN to be, and (2) what the management style of the organization is.

9.1 The Influence of Organizational Perception of LANs

Some organizations see LANs as an evolutionary technology. It is the latest in the chain of technological developments in data communications, providing high-speed data communications over considerable distances.[50] Others go a step further and see LANs in the context of distributed systems. According to Liebowitz [124], LANs can be viewed as having a modest level of cooperation between communicating devices over a relatively close geographical separation. This evolutionary approach sees the purpose of LANs to provide data communication between devices; in particular, to allow computers to communicate with one another and to share storage and printing facilities. Additionally, the evolutionary approach sees the growth of LANs as natural and necessary given the burgeoning use of microcomputers. In fact, most of the LANs available seem to mirror this philosophy, e.g. Econet, Omninet, HiNet, Cluster/One, etc. ARC, the Datapoint network, is very similar except that instead of allowing the interconnections of micros, it was designed for the interconnection of minicomputers.

This evolutionary approach to LANs is interesting in the sense that it is hard to say why these LANs are not local computer networks. Actually, they are, and it is important that an organization realizes what it is buying when it purchases one of the above-mentioned products. That is, these LANs are mechanisms to interconnect computers and their related equipment. Text processing and distribution—in that text is treated as data—is also handled by the LANs. They do not, however, allow for any video or voice processing. In the evolutionary approach, local area networks and local computer networks are not usually differentiated. Often they are described under the generic term 'local network' or are lumped together under local area networks.[51]

There exists a second approach which does differentiate between local computer networks and LANs and views local area networks more as a revolutionary technology. This view asserts that the primary function of a LAN is to link all forms of information generating devices together, thus permitting data, text, voice, and video interconnection and communication. Organizations holding this view of LANs would very likely see LANs in terms of linking together the various technologies of office automation. Office automation would also be seen in a somewhat revolutionary light.

Given that LANs are seen in terms of linking voice, video, text, and data, those products mentioned above, e.g. Econet, Omninet, etc., would not be accepted as LANs, only as LCNs. Unfortunately, any organization looking for this kind of LAN would be disappointed—there are none at present. The closest an organization could get would be SILK which handles voice as well as data and text or WangNet which handles video, data, and text. SILK is a baseband system which would offer little possibility of adding video. WangNet, on the other hand, is a broadband system and could have the potential of dealing with voice traffic as well (although at the moment this feature is far from becoming reality). Xerox's advertisement of the 'information outlet' where various kinds of information technology, e.g. printers, copiers, workstations, etc., communicate with one another by just plugging them in to some form of ring main is still more fiction than fact. Xerox's approach to the 'information ring main'—Ethernet—handles data and text but not voice or video. Ethernet is however more sophisticated than a local computer network in that it allows the connection of devices such as intelligent copiers, management workstations, and the like.

For those organizations viewing LANs as a revolutionary technology, the LAN products available will seem disappointing. Organizations in this camp will have to be wary about developing plans which include local area networks that allow the interconnection of voice, video, text and, data technological devices.

There is something of a third alternative approach to LANs adopted by some organizations which is neither evolutionary nor revolutionary but is more of a combination of the two. It might be termed 'evolutionary-revolution' or 'random-convergence'. This is the realization that LANs are not the homogeneous technology which many write about. And although the ultimate goal of LANs is to allow four previous unrelated technologies to be merged, i.e. voice, video, data, and text—a revolutionary idea—it has come about in a rather random and disparate fashion. LANs are very much more heterogeneous than most realize.

'Random-convergence' is not a notion tied strictly to local area networks or information technology. In an interesting case study Emery and Trist [125] recounted the history of one organization where seemingly random or chance events occurring over time converged to cause the organization serious problems. Emery and Trist discussed this phenomenon in terms of 'environmental connectedness' but this is very similar to the notion of 'random-convergence'.

The case study centred on a post-war British canned food company whose major product was tinned vegetables. The company planned to expand its operation by building a modern automated factory at the cost of several million pounds. The company had commanded a lion's share of the market (65%) and saw no reason why this would change.

Before the factory could even be completed, a series of apparently detached and random events overtook the planned future of the company. When all the factors converged together they made the modern factory totally uneconomic and unnecessary. The order of events was as follows. Owing to the ending of wartime controls on steel strip and tin, a number of new small canning firms emerged. Their main product was imported fruit. At first, there appeared to be no conflict with the expanding vegetable canning company. However, in an effort to keep their machinery and labour employed in the off-season, the small fruit canners looked for other means by which this could be done. The US quick-frozen food industry provided an answer. Much of the US vegetable crop was unsuitable for the frozen food industry but could be used in canning. Since the American farmers had been selling these crops cheaply as animal feed, they were happy and eager to sell them to the new small British canners at a higher price. This mutually advantageous agreement allowed the new canners to undercut the large vegetable canning company. Further, underdeveloped countries exacerbated the vegetable canner's problems by offering to sell their crops to the small canners more cheaply.

Concomitant with the company's problems in the supply market were problems in its product market. Whereas previously a high-quality tinned vegetable product held the top of the market, the quick-frozen products were beginning to supplant this dominance. Because of post-war affluence, frozen vegetables took over the high-quality end of the market leaving the tinned foods with the middle and lower ends. Further, the lower end of the market was quickly absorbed by the small canners. The introduction in Britain of the supermarket and chain store posed a new and devastating complication for the vegetable canning company. The supermarket, wanting to enhance their image and increase their share of the tinned vegetable market, sought to establish low-priced house brands. Prior to the war, the house brands accounted for less than 1% of the market; this rose to 50% after the war. Much of the growth was at the expense of the large vegetable canners.

All of the aforementioned events combined to make the consequences of building the new factory deleterious. The company's management had failed to appreciate that a number of seemingly random events were converging to invalidate their reasons for planned expansion. The company tried desperately to protect its old market share—and the new factory—without success. 'Random-convergence' had taken its toll.

The following are a few examples upon which the random-convergence approach to LANs is based. Dow Chemicals [126] of Midland, Michigan, developed their own local area network to handle video transmission and for process control and monitoring. They developed a broadband system that had six video channels which were used for employee education programmes, news, weather, safety programmes, and the like. Other channels were used by Dow's process control computers to monitor remote equipment. More recently, Dow added an energy management system onto the network. Additionally, they have made use of the network for data communications—particularly remote job entry and VDU terminal communication to the mainframe—which has proven the versatility of this LAN concept. Here is an example of a LAN whose primary and original purpose was video communication but has developed into much more.

The private automatic branch exchange (PABX) or the so-called 'intelligent switch' is another aspect of the random-convergence approach to LANs. PABXs are computer-based telephone switching devices. At present they are mostly used for automatic dialling, re-routing of calls, automatic call back, audio conferencing, voice store and forward, and so on. But in the future one can foresee their possible handling of more than just voice. In fact, a number of PABX products are being announced which will additionally handle data and text with the telephone handset being used as a data terminal. Whether a future PABX-type system is capable of video communication is unanswerable at present, but this possibility cannot be ruled out. Here is another example of a product developed for a specific purpose, i.e. voice communication, but which has now been recognized as having the potential to cover the whole range of information technology intercommunication.

Other examples of the heterogeneity of LANs abound. SILK is a local area network which is equally capable of handling voice and data. LocalNet is a broadband LAN which has the capability of video signalling but is really only set up for data traffic. Video transmission is available because of the high bandwidth on this broadband system yet seems to be advertised only because of the spare capacity on the coaxial cable. Hyperchannel offers a very high data rate (50 Mbps) but that is because it was developed as a processor-to-processor interconnecting system. It has the potential to provide other than just data transmission but it is not clear who will use it. WangNet is designed to handle video, text, and data communications equally. Given Wang's heavy involvement in word processors and office systems, this type of LAN support seems the most appropriate.

Those organizations viewing LANs from a random-convergence point of view may find the LAN marketplace less confusing and have a better understanding of why the various LAN products are what they are and how they might develop in the future. These organizations are less likely to be left behind by LAN technology nor be fooled into believing the 'information outlet' has arrived.

9.2 The Influence of Management Style

A second factor which could very likely play a key role in the way a LAN affects an organization is that of management style or philosophy. By management style is meant the overall approach adopted by an organization to managing and controlling its resources. It is often described in terms of a 'centralized' or 'decentralized' policy. Burns and Stalker [127] referred to it in terms of an organization being 'mechanistic' or 'organic'. Others have discussed it in terms of 'degree of bureaucratization' [128], and so on. To simplify somewhat what are really rather complicated ideas expressed in these various descriptions, management style may be described as a policy of management which can be classified along a continuum of centralization to decentralization. Centralization is the characteristic of organizations which are more hierarchically structured, with a formal chain of command and might normally be referred to as highly bureaucratic.[52] Decentralization refers to those organizations which are not very hierarchically structured, have fewer formal chains of command, allow for more local autonomy, and are not considered bureaucratic.

Which form of management style is appropriate to which organization, in what time frame, and for what purposes, have been research questions for organizational theorists for some time. What is relevant for the discussion of LAN implementation in organizations is whether a LAN philosophy of distributed intelligence and information processing is appropriate for organizations which have a centralized management style. In these organizations, information flow is mostly upwards, with control channelled mostly downwards. Local area networks, on the other hand, have the potential for allowing much more vertical communication. This would come about through passing of messages from one management workstation or micro to another through the LAN. (Note also that LANs could have a dramatic effect on horizontal communication as well.)

According to Hiltz and Turoff [130] the amount of communication between individuals can increase quite dramatically after they become familiar with the specific means of communication. In their study the means of communication was a computer-based message passing system called EIES. Thus one might expect the amount of communication between individuals—particularly at the same level of organization—to increase. This might be acceptable—indeed desirable—in organizations which have a decentralized management style, but potentially problematic in more centralized organizations.

A second aspect associated with management style and its relationship to LANs is that of control. Centralized organizations usually have fairly strong and well defined control structures and mechanisms which allow the organization to be centrally controlled. LANs make this control more difficult because of the new channels of communication possible with LANs. Additionally there is the issue of the distribution of data with a LAN. LANs permit data to be distributed in many locations, thus making it more difficult to exercise central control.

A third aspect of LANs involves the kinds of communication possible. LANs permit the linking of voice, image, data, and text, thus creating a number of powerful communication potentials. The skillful use of such mixed communication media could lead to a whole new range of propaganda materials and thereby altering existing organizational power balances. It is not clear whether the ability of LANs to support new kinds of communication possibilities would be more effective in centralized or decentralized organizations, but one could envisage cases where this, in combination with distributed data, could lessen the influence of senior management in centralized organizations.

In sum, LANs are a technology for distributed processing. The arguments for and against distributed processing are well known and not really the subject of this text. Nevertheless, it is clear that the implications of a distributed technology—LANs in this case—has much to do with the management style or philosophy of the organization. It appears somewhat incongruous to think about organizations which are highly structured, centralized, and bureaucratic using distributed processing technology, unless the organization was attempting to change its style. Similarly, the use of LANs should be considered in this context. Heavily centralized organizations would perhaps be better off using some form of star or hierarchical controlled network if they wish some form of device interconnection. This provides them with basically a centrally controlled solution, mirroring their management style. LANs, alternatively, may well be a better solution to those organizations which have a more decentralized style or philosophy; distributed processing to mirror distributed organizational control.

There is one further issue somewhat related to the issue of management style, as described above, and that is the PABX-controlled network alternative.

LANs, as have been shown, are a distributed processing solution to the problem of device interconnection. LANs have in some senses evolved mostly around the need to transmit and receive data. Voice, image, and text are often thought of in terms of being variations of data. Thus, it was natural to expect and then to see LAN products being developed mostly by computer companies. Computer companies have historically produced products for data processing. And the movement from LCNs to LANs was done either to generate a new market or to develop a product to fill a market need. The market is, of course, office automation. Yet the question which must be asked is how appropriate is it to look at voice, image, and text as variations of data? And can a technology designed for data really adequately handle the other three? Given the lack of available products, no satisfactory answer can be given to the latter question. The former is, however, somewhat answerable. In the sense that voice, image, and text can be digitized they can all be viewed or thought of as data. Yet digitized voice and image generate enormous quantities of data and it must be questioned whether this is the most appropriate way to see the four technologies, i.e. as all variants of data. An alternative view is that of the PABX-controlled network.

PABXs, as was described earlier, are computer-based telephone switching devices which are becoming more sophisticated every day. Initially, they dealt only with voice but a number are being announced which will handle data and text as well. The telephone handset will be transformed into a data terminal. In this case, data and text are perceived as variants of voice. The PABX (or integrated branch exchange) controlled network is a real alternative to the LAN. The PABX acts as the controller and hub of the network, and provides a gateway to other networks, e.g. public data networks, value added networks, the public telephone network, private services, etc.

In comparing the two approaches, LAN vs. PABX, a number of interesting differences emerge. First, there are more LAN or LAN-type products available than there are PABX-controlled networks. In fact, there really are no PABX-controlled networks available which are anywhere near as sophisticated as the LAN products. Nevertheless, with industry giants such as AT&T, Bell Northern, Plessey, and the like, could such products be that far away? Secondly, LANs are a distributed solution to the interconnection problem; PABX systems are a centralized solution. Based on the arguments made above, certain organizations may find this style of technology more acceptable as it more closely parallels their organizational philosophies. Thirdly, LANs have been described as a computer vendor designed solution to the problem of interconnection. As such, mean time between failures (of the LAN) may be thought of in terms of what might be acceptable in terms of computer failure. In computer terms, a mean time between failures of once or twice a year might be acceptable. However, a LAN which was handling an organization's data, text, telephone (voice), and video traffic might need to have a mean time between failures of once in every three, four or more years to be considered acceptable. What would happen if an organization found all its telephones and video monitoring systems down for an extended period. Quite often people can live with computer systems going down for one reason or another—it is a common feature in our lives. However, people might not be so willing to part with their telephone or video system. PABXs have so far shown themselves to be remarkably robust. Their mean time between failures is very high indeed.

Whether this will continue to be the case once they become sophisticated enough to handle data, text, and video, cannot be determined. One final point on the PABX-controlled alternative, the centralized nature of this approach may make it attractive to IBM—particularly as it mirrors IBM's philosophy towards data processing. This alternative might turn out to be the most natural for IBM and thus garner strong IBM support.

The PABX-controlled network might turn out to be a viable alternative to a LAN approach, particularly for those organizations who prefer a more centrally controlled approach to interconnection. But without products by which to assess this alternative, the LAN may win by default.

Chapter 10

An Implementation Approach for LANs

Local area networks are an important piece of technology. The ability to interconnect voice, image, text, and data will no doubt lead to a whole new range of communication possibilities. Even the concept of an office and its relationship to work could be dramatically altered. (See for example the research done by Olson [131] on remote office work, and others who have speculated about the impact of office automation on office workers [130,132–135].) Thus, local area networks, as the glue which holds the technologies of office automation together, are of paramount importance. Yet very little has been written about implementing office automation, let alone LANs. The little which has been written about office automation implementation is usually of a superficial nature and/or not relevant to LAN implementation.

The need to consider how an organization implements a LAN is important as a LAN can have serious consequences on organizational activities (see the previous chapter on the organizational implications of LANs). These organizational activities are human in nature, i.e. performed largely by individuals, and it is therefore important to consider the human and behavioural dimension in LAN implementation.

This is not a new idea. There is a whole body of knowledge subsumed under the rubric of 'implementation research' which grew up largely out of the need to understand why so many management science models and computer-based systems had failed to achieve their objectives in the 1960s and early 1970s.[53] (See for example, Lucas [136] whose dramatic accounts of information systems failures sparked off much research into implementation issues.) Interest in research on implementation has surged over the past few years giving rise to a number of conferences on the subject and numerous papers in the journals. Some of the discussion on implementation has even come from unusual sources. For example, in a study on the superior performance of Japanese firms, Howard [137] reports that one of the reasons for their success is the great emphasis the Japanese place on implementation. It is a primary

117

consideration in their planning process. Owens [138] concurs with the need to plan for implementation. He writes:

> Successful implementation depends on a match between user needs and systems design. This match is achieved through assessment of organizational and individual variables affecting implementation outcomes. Such an assessment requires extensive planning.

Ginzberg [139] also agrees. He sees the importance of implementation research lying in the fact that 'we are still better able to develop models and design systems than to get those models and systems used by people in organisations'. His recommendation on implementation is an approach based on the Kolb-Frohman model of the consulting process.

There have been a number of implementation approaches advocated in the literature, but unfortunately the issue of which implementation approach is best cannot be answered concretely. It would, of course, depend on certain organizational characteristics and realities. Nevertheless, implementation research has led to two important conclusions which appear to be true in all circumstances:

(1) implementation is a process rather than a product,
(2) the behavioural aspects of the change process must be considered and managed.

Implementation, to be meaningful and successful, must consider the behavioural dimension as well as the technical dimension when implementing or introducing new information technology.

10.1 The Socio-Technical Systems Approach

The concept of jointly considering and 'optimizing' both the technical and social components of implementation is precisely the philosophy of the socio-technical systems (STS) approach, and is embodied within the implementation approach recommended here.

The STS approach sees any technological intervention, e.g. information systems/technology implementation, as having two components: the technical system involving various job tasks and technology; and the social system involving people with their various roles, behaviours, etc. These two systems must be separated from one another, initially, to determine the requirements of each. Once these have been ascertained, the STS process proceeds by recombining the variables in each system in such a way that the two systems are ultimately jointly optimized. Bostrom [140] discussed this point succinctly:

> The goal of joint optimization implies the best design alternatives in the technical system and their affects on having the best in the social system are jointly considered. Technical system optimization is usually measured in terms of improvement in task accomplishment (i.e. improvements in productivity) while social system optimization is measured in terms of gains in the quality of working life of the work system's members (i.e. improvements in the ability of employees

to satisfy their personal needs, e.g. meaningful and satisfying work, recognition, control and influence, learning opportunities, good wages and working conditions, and the like).

Mumford [141] defines the socio-technical systems approach as 'a design philosophy that produces productivity, quality, coordination, and control; but also provides a work environment and task structure in which people can achieve personal development and satisfaction.

10.2 Participation—Issues

One of the more popular ways of implementing an STS philosophy is through participative systems design and implementation involving the employees who will eventually have to operate and use the new work system [141]. Mumford offers four principal arguments for the use of participation: (1) that individuals have a moral right to control, as much as possible, their own destinies and this includes any new technology/system which may affect them; (2) that activities are ultimately controlled by those who perform them, and people who do not have a say in these decisions about activities, may choose not to abide by them; (3) that the most knowledge and expertise on any given operational task is possessed by those people performing the task; and (4) that involvement of individuals acts as a motivation and will therefore lead to higher productivity and more efficiency. (See Hedberg [142] for an excellent treatment on the case for participation in systems implementation.)

There are many forms of participation and various ways in which a participative approach could be implemented. Land [143] describes three broad categories of participation:

(1) *Consultative*—This is where the participants provide input into the systems design process but where the bulk of the decisions are left to some other group, e.g. systems analysts. Ideally, the grounds on which the various decisions were reached should be published for the participants to see. In this situation, participation is often confined to particular special interest groups identified as being affected by the proposed system/technology introduction. Normally the kind of input provided by the participants is limited to social system considerations such as job satisfaction needs.

(2) *Democratic*—This is where all the participants have an equal voice in the decisions affecting systems development or at least in the decision-making process. The implementation of decisions, however, is left in the hands of some other group or authority, e.g. senior management. To summarize, the participants make the decisions, but it is left up to another group, e.g. senior management, to approve and make sure they are implemented.

(3) *Responsible*—This is where the participants not only make the decisions but also assume full responsibility and authority for their implementa-

tion. In this situation all workers who will use the new system or technology are involved, on a continuous basis, in the development and implementation process. This approach has been described by some as the only true form of participation.

Mumford [141] describes a classification scheme of participation types which is similar to that of Land's. Her scheme differs from Land's in that she sees one form of participation based on representation. That is, a group of workers is elected to represent the needs of their fellow workers in the development and implementation process. This group tries to ensure the new work system provides both high job satisfaction and high efficiency.

Both authors imply that the 'responsible' (Mumford refers to it as 'consensus') form of participation is the ideal, but that certain situations and environments may militate against this form of participation in favour of some other. Since all organizations are different, no one best form of participation exists. Rather, participation has to be considered in the light of existing organizational realities.

The participative approach to LAN implementation, it is felt, would have much to offer. LAN implementation could act as a catalyst in getting the various organizational users of the technology thinking about the new social arrangements possible. Remote work, new group and work structures, new activities, and the like are all facilitated by LAN introduction. Given that organizational members know most about their activities and the tasks they perform, they are in the best position to say what types of arrangements will be best for them. Additionally, any new technology being introduced has a better chance of success (and being used) if its users understand the technology and feel they are in some sense responsible for its introduction. Participation allows for this. Thus, the value of participation in LAN implementation would seem to be obvious.

10.2.1 Specifying the aspects of participation

Although participation in LAN implementation has almost universal acceptance as a key aspect of implementation, few offer any structural way for participation to take place. Most assume that implementors of the technology should involve the users but fail to specify: the form of participation, the content of participation, the degree of participation, the groups who should be involved, the stages at which participation should take place, and so on. Yet, these aspects are important and could very well affect the value of participation.

10.2.1.1 Form

There are two forms of participation:

(a) direct form,
(b) indirect form.

Direct form is when each user who has to use the technology, or will be affected, can take part in its discussion. In the indirect form, this is done on behalf of the user by some representative.

10.2.1.2 Content

There are basically three types of content on which participation can take place:

(a) long range,
(b) tactical decision making,
(c) operational tasks.

Participation associated with the long-term survival of the firm, with its ownership, nature of corporate control, etc., is considered to be in category (a). Participation in tactical decisions such as the hiring of managers, setting budgets, or the decision to use office automation would fall into category (b). Participation in operational activities, i.e. those activities which directly affect an employee's task performance and/or working life, is of the category (c) variety.

10.2.1.3 Degree

This is basically the degree to which participation can influence the actual decision. As was described earlier, Land [143] classified degree of participation in terms of:

(a) consultative,
(b) democratic,
(c) responsible.

10.2.1.4 The groups involved

There have been a number of frameworks by which to categorize the various users of a specific system or technology, but one useful way is to classify user groups as follows.

(a) *Primary users*—These are users who work directly and internally with the system/technology. They have the ability to modify and mould the system/technology while being responsible for its effective and efficient running and operation. They have the job of trying to keep the other users happy. Examples of primary users are computer programmers and analysts.

(b) *Secondary users*—These are users who work more indirectly with the system. They provide input to and/or receive output from the system/technology, but have no power (ability) to change it directly. They can, however, influence its operation by indirect means, e.g. asking the programmers and/or analysts to change part of the system/technology. Examples of secondary users are bank clerks and tellers, who work with an online banking system, and secretaries who use word processors.

(c) *Tertiary users*—These are users who do not interact with the system/technology, but are nevertheless affected by it. They may receive some reports from the system, but they work neither directly nor indirectly with the system. A tertiary user also has no direct way of influencing the system's/technology's operation. He may write a letter to a manager, who in turn may request some change, but his ability to change the system is very limited. An example of tertiary users would be a firm's customers. They receive bills, invoices, etc., from the system, but have little ability to make changes.

10.2.1.5 The stages at which it should take place

Any system or technology must go through a number of stages from the time there is perceived to be a problem, to the time the technology/system is implemented, to the time the system/technology is considered out of date and in need of replacement. Often these stages are discussed in terms of the system's life cycle and involve:

(1) project selection,
(2) feasibility study,
(3) systems analysis,
(4) logical systems design,
(5) physical systems design,
(6) implementation,
(7) maintenance,
(8) review and assessment.

10.2.2 Discussion on essential features of participation

Clearly there could never be one type of participation which would be satisfactory in all cases. Each situation is unique and has its own essential features that need to be taken into account. One way to look at some of these unique features is to classify them into three separate headings.

10.2.2.1 Participation potential of the organization

This is the potential of the organization to allow participation to occur, and is based more on the macro-organizational and environmental issues. It assumes organizations are entities in their own right and possess a number of contextual characteristics, e.g. size, history, structure, age, technical system, and so on.

Additionally, the environment of an organization is also viewed as important. The environment can be thought to consist of the following [144]:

(1) physical structure,
(2) social structure,
(3) ecological structure,
(4) legal structure,
(5) cultural structure,
(6) political structure,
(7) economic structure,
(8) psychological structure,
(9) international structure.

It may be classified as simple or complex and/or stable or dynamic.

In general, organizations which have a more decentralized and autonomous structure, have a history of worker participation in decision making, and are more concerned with the growth in industrial democracy, will have a high potential for participation in LAN implementation.

10.2.2.2   User propensity to it

Not all people may want to participate. Participation may be considered to be related to responsibility. The more one participates, the higher the level of responsibility. It has been shown that some people do not necessarily want responsibilities or increases in responsibility. Others may want the responsibility but are not capable of participating. Lawrence [145] asks how do you force or teach people to participate? This is not a skill possessed or even understood by all. Telling a person to participate does not mean that 'true' participation will occur. Thus, user propensity to participate will depend on individual factors such as: attitude, perceived power, perceived value, group pressures, knowledge of the subject, interest in the subject, and the like.

In general, users are often found to be willing and wanting to participate, but sometimes lacking the proper knowledge of what to do. Therefore, a bit of pretraining on the various aspects of participation and local area networks might be advantageous.

10.2.2.3   Management acceptance of it

Not all managers/superiors are agreeable to sharing their decision-making power. Managerial ideology, values, philosophies, etc., are often at odds with what participation is trying to accomplish. Thus, it is not uncommon to find reticence on the part of management when it comes to participation. Again, the acceptance of participation will depend on their attitudes, capabilities, perceived value, pressures, and the like.

In general, management acceptance of participation is something which can be fostered, but it often needs a catalyst and a sponsor: someone or something to start the process, and someone who is willing to see the participation exercise through to fruition. Management acceptance of particpation is the key variable if participation, as an organizational approach to LAN implementation, is to be successful.

10.2.3 Desirability of some aspects of participation

Turning now to the five aspects of participation cited earlier, it can be seen that certain types of participation might be more desirable than others when implementing LANs.

10.2.3.1 Form

It is felt that the direct form of participation would be more beneficial in the long run than the indirect form. LANs can dramatically alter the work and tasks that their users perform. Given that most people are somewhat fearful of change—based on not knowing what the future will hold—it is not uncommon to expect and to find resistance to change [145]. A direct form of participation would do much to mitigate the fear as the users would understand much more about LANs and thus be less inclined to resist their introduction. Indirect participation—if the direct form is not acceptable to the organization's management—is better than no participation, but one must be wary of labels such as manipulation and non-representation in indirect participation. (See Hedberg [146] for a good treatment on some of the possible dysfunctional consequences of using an indirect form of participation.)

10.2.3.2 Content

Participation in LAN implementation, it is felt, should be concerned more with operational tasks and tactical decision making than long-range (or strategic) activities. That is, the content of participation should centre around the more non-strategic activities because most use of the LAN would be made by clerical people and managers. Different organizations, however, might have different thoughts on what the content of participation should be. Some might feel that participation in LAN implementation should be restricted to operational activities only, i.e. those activities which directly affect an employee's task performance. Others might feel that participation should be centred around tactical decision making, for example whether to implement a LAN or not. Once having decided that a particular technology is appropriate its implementation is left to the professionals—the DP department, etc. Yet even though these different approaches to the content of participation exist, it is felt that participation in LAN implementation should embrace both tactical actions and operational activities.

10.2.3.3 Degree

Ideally, the degree of participation should be one of 'responsible', i.e. the participants not only make the decisions about LAN implementation but also assume full responsibility and authority over the carrying-out of the decisions. It is based on the assumption that only if the participants have responsibility and authority will they feel that true participation has taken place. And true participation is the most likely way to ensure that the full support of the users is obtained, thus lessening any prospect of sabotage, resistance, avoidance or other dysfunctional behaviour. Should 'responsible' participation not be possible, then the next best alternative is 'democratic', where all participants have an equal voice in LAN implementation but exercise no authority or responsibility over its outcome. And if this is not possible, then the 'consultative' degree of participation is recommended. This is based on the maxim: 'some participation is better than no participation'.

10.2.3.4 The groups involved

It might be argued that all three groups of users, i.e. primary, secondary, and tertiary, should be involved in the participation in LAN implementation. However, the tertiary users—in the main—would be far less affected by the LAN than the other two groups. Additionally, it would be difficult to have this group participating in LAN implementation. Therefore it is felt that the primary and secondary users should be involved in the participation exercise, with perhaps some input by representatives of the tertiary users. Identifying all primary and secondary users might not be easy, but this identification is important and is worth the time which is needed.

10.2.3.5 The stages at which it should take place

Research has shown that participation is most valuable at the early stages of the system's life cycle, i.e. project selection, feasibility, systems analysis, and logical design, although participation would obviously be of value in the review and assessment stage. In the case of LAN implementation, the same would also be true. Most participation would occur in the beginning when deciding whether to implement a LAN, what type of LAN, what changes in structural arrangements to make, and so on. Participation would slacken, the further into the system's life cycle the LAN progressed.

10.3 Participation—How?

One of the great difficulties associated with participation is 'how?'. Most recognize its value, but are unsure of how to structure the participation so that it is meaningful. For example, most users—outside the DP department—are not particularly knowledgeable about technical matters, and would find difficulty in determining technical requirements. Similarly, the systems analysts and programmers would have difficulty in determining and analysing social structure requirements for the users of the technology. The solution is to have two groups (as was suggested in the discussion in Section 10.2.3.4), one group for the primary users, a second group for the secondary users. The secondary users would presumably be the non-technical people and would

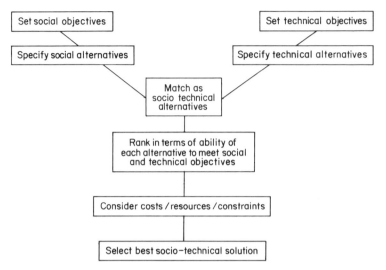

Fig. 21. Participation leading to a socio-technical solution.

specifically consider the social requirements and alternatives. The primary users, from the data processing department, would consider the technical requirements and alternatives. These two sets of requirements and alternatives would then be matched and evaluated. The result would be an acceptable socio-technical solution.[54] Fig. 21, which has been adapted from Mumford and Weir [147], depicts the process diagrammatically.

10.4   Other Aspects of the LAN Implementation Approach

In addition to the participative process used to implement a socio-technical system solution described here, there are a number of other aspects which need to be specified. The following is a list of additional recommendations based on the current state of implementation research knowledge which, if followed, should help lead to successful LAN implementation.

10.4.1   Recognize the need for a facilitator

A facilitator is someone who can help the participation exercise along. At times the participative approach can get bogged down: people not knowing what to do next, what issues to consider, in what order, and so on. The facilitator should act to keep participation occurring smoothly. Also, the facilitator can act in a liaison capacity between the various groups and can help in the matching of social with technical alternatives.[55] The role of the facilitator is often likened to that of a change agent as it is described in the organizational development literature.

10.4.2 Involve all affected groups

The participative approach should involve all affected users in the setting of objectives, priorities, needs, and problems.[56] It is important to recognize that, if certain individuals who may be affected by LAN implementation are not involved in the participative process, various priorities, problem perceptions, needs, etc., may be biased. Quite often organizational objectives, when translated down into departmental objectives, have become distorted, or worse, contradictory between departments. The classic example is the sales department who want a high inventory level and the accounting department who try to minimize the level of inventory because of the carrying costs, etc. Other examples abound. Thus, it is imperative that *all* affected parties are involved in LAN implementation.

10.4.3 Assign responsibilities and clarify commitments

There is a need to have all participating groups and individuals aware of their responsibilities ahead of time. This implies that the participants are assigned responsibilities for LAN implementation. As was mentioned earlier, responsibilities help to guarantee that the individual's involvement in the participation exercise is meaningful. Commitments in terms of time, effort, budget, and sundry must also be clarified at the outset. Participants must be aware of what the exercise will involve and be under no delusions about its simplicity or the amount of time and effort needed.

10.4.4 A realistic plan of action must be developed

The participative approach is a time-consuming activity. Thus it is imperative that realistic timetables, level of work estimates, and budgets for each participative activity are worked out. It must be borne in mind that most of the time-consuming activities will occur at the initial stages. This time will be made up by the shorter lead time to getting the LAN totally operative and used by the various organizational members. That is, participation lessens the amount of formal training needed and there would be less reticence on the part of the users in using the LAN.

10.4.5 Senior management support must be explicit

Senior management must be seen to be staunchly behind the participative approach and interested in the LAN implementation. Explicit support is a necessary but not sufficient condition for participation to be successful. Senior management's support must be highly visible in more than just a lukewarm or animated fashion. Participation will be most successful when there is perceived to be sincere interest on the part of senior management. And given the importance and potential serious dysfunctional consequences of deficient

LAN implementation and use, senior management support should be relatively easy to enlist.

10.4.6 Establish rewards to encourage the development and utilization of the LAN

A local area network is a new technology which can change the nature of work and what people do in the office. As such, a natural reaction on the part of the people who must use the technology is to be somewhat fearful and resistant to the change. Participation in LAN implementation has been described as potentially the most useful vehicle for minimizing fear and resistance. An additional way to get people interested in and using LANs is to provide institutional rewards for LAN use. These rewards could take on many different forms depending on organizational circumstances and should not be limited to the monetary variety. All rewards should be designed to encourage LAN use and should not embrace sanctions against those who are not so inclined.

10.4.7 Develop a clear picture of the level of dependence of the LAN users on the LAN

It must be recognized from the outset that some people will not want to use a LAN no matter what the rewards, sanctions, etc. Alternatively, some will use the LAN for purposes which were not (and perhaps could not be) conceived of initially. Others, will use a LAN in some circumstances, but not others. It is therefore important to obtain a picture of the level of dependence that various users will have on the LAN, and its alternatives. If a high level of LAN use is required, then all alternatives to the LAN would need to be eliminated, i.e. make the users very dependent on the LAN. However, a high level of LAN use caused by a high level of user dependence does not mean that the users are necessarily happy with the LAN. High use does not necessarily mean high satisfaction. Thus, level of dependence and alternative possibilities should be recognized.

10.4.8 Group and individual needs, motivations, pressures, etc., will have a great impact on LAN implementation

The history of computing is rife with examples of computer systems which were built and introduced only to find they were not used because the social elements were not fully considered. Much of this section has been devoted to this very point. The use of participation within the context of socio-technical system development has been proposed as the most appropriate way to deal with these social elements. Yet, participation is not enough. There is a need for all to realize that successful LAN implementation and use is contingent upon a myriad of social aspects. For example, an individual may not use a LAN, even though he may have participated in its implementation, if his peers perceive LAN use as not acceptable. Group pressures—based on group norms and values—are very powerful forces and must be recognized and somehow dealt with. It is therefore advisable that agreements be made, in advance, so as to lessen pressures arising out of uncertainties. Additionally, organizations should set up procedures and mechanisms to resolve conflicts arising out of group and individual pressures on LAN implementation and use.

10.5 Some Additional Implementation Issues Associated With LAN Use

The implementation approach and recommendations described so far should lead to successful introduction and use of LANs in organizations. However, there are a few additional points—arising out of the office automation literature—which should be considered when implementing a LAN.

10.5.1 A certain level of LAN use must be maintained

A certain level of LAN usage is needed on a regular basis in order for the user to maintain his willingness and ability to use the system. Local area networks are, in the words of Curley and Pyburn [150], 'an intelligent technology' rather than an 'industrial technology'. And because of this, the kind of learning necessary to have LANs used will be different. According to Curley and Pyburn, 'industrial technologies—engines, aircraft, and the like— require a much greater proportion of learning time devoted to training' and rather less to something they described as 'adaptive, ongoing'. 'Adaptive, ongoing' refers to a kind of learning different from training which one acquires over time with the constant use of a specific technology. By using the technology over some period of time, a user begins to see uses of the technology not initially considered.) 'Intellectual technologies' require a much greater proportion of time devoted to this 'adaptive, ongoing' type of learning.

10.5.2 A user's peers must be LAN users as well

In addition to the social pressures of peer groups and co-workers on an individual either to use or not to use a specific technology, there is another aspect associated with peers, viz. their own use of the LAN. That is, for an individual to want to use a LAN, his peers and co-workers must be using it as well. This is because most of his use of the LAN will be in the form of communication with his peers and co-workers. Thus, if they are not using the LAN, he will have little reason to use it.

10.5.3 The LAN must be readily available to anyone who wants to use it

Bair [151] has shown that, for a technology to be properly utilized, it needs to be available to each individual who wants to use it at all times during his working day. Bair claims that if this is not the case, problems and dysfunctional consequences will arise. Thought must be given to who will want to use a LAN when it is implemented, and how easy it will be for those individuals actually to have access to it. It must be remembered that availability of a LAN of itself may not be sufficient; the LAN should be *readily* available.

10.6 Summary

This section has attempted to show that LAN implementation is a very important issue to consider. If LANs are not implemented properly, their value may be limited indeed. Therefore, this section has drawn heavily on the principles of implementation research to offer an approach to LAN implementation based on socio-technical systems concepts and participation. The result, it is hoped, is an approach which will lead to the successful implementation and subsequent use of local area networks.

Concluding Remarks

Local area networks are one of the more interesting and potentially revolutionary technologies to be developed of late. Yet the confusion surrounding LANs has been very great indeed. This text has hopefully lessened the confusion, as the various concepts, issues, and approaches associated with LANs have been discussed. A word of caution must be added however. The technology of LANs is progressing very rapidly. New LAN products are seemingly introduced on an almost weekly basis. Standards discussion continues at a relentless pace. Research on LAN performance, integrity, reliability, etc., is churning out statistics which have to be analysed and dealt with. And the list runs on and on. The point is: much of the current knowledge about LANs will become dated relatively quickly—as is the case in any burgeoning technological area. Thus, the reader who wishes to keep abreast of the developments in LANs will be required to do extensive and continuous reading . . . happy reading!

PART III: APPENDICES

Appendix A

A Brief Note on the Effect of Collision Control Algorithms (CCA) on the Performance of CSMA-CD

The employment of any contention protocol means that collisions are inevitable. Attempts to reduce the number of collisions and consequently improve performance have included modifications to CSMA-CD by assigning transmission priorities, grouping competing stations, and the provision of collision cycles. Thus, the performance the CSMA-CD protocol is closely related to the CCA employed.

The binary exponential back-off (BEB) algorithm tries to minimize the probability of repeated collisions by selecting a retransmission delay from a random number interval. This interval is doubled with each successive collision. The doubling process is terminated after ten consecutive retransmission attempts (referred to as truncated BEB) and any subsequent attempts remain at this interval until transmission is aborted. The truncation of the retransmission delay is a function of the number of stations on the subnetwork, i.e. on the Ethernet doubling is truncated at ten because the maximum number of stations is 1024 [33].

BEB assumes that a particular packet colliding a number of times is due to heavy traffic on the subnetwork. Thus, it was considered desirable to impose a longer retransmission delay so that the load in the immediate future is reduced. Hence, a possible weakness in BEB is the rapid increase in retransmission delay with a corresponding increase in the number of collisions and, because of this, CCAs of a less reactive nature have been proposed.

Simply expressed, polynomial back-off (PB) offers an alternative algorithm to schedule retransmissions by multiplying the propagation delay of the system by a certain factor. This factor is also related to the number of collisions, but does not involve any doubling, merely the multiplication of the interval by an incremented factor. The linear incremental back-off (LIB) algorithm is one of the simplest of the PB algorithms. Simulation studies have demonstrated that the LIB algorithms attempt to resolve conflicts without the imposition of high cost in terms of retransmission delay and, in doing so, yield better performance characteristics than BEB [37].

The fixed mean back-off (FMB) algorithm is another variation of PB, where the mean retransmission delay is not related to the number of collisions but is a constant. The determination of the constant is that value which would produce the optimal performance. If the value of the constant is insufficiently large, too many repetitive collisions would result before successful transmission. Conversely, excessive valuation of the constant will mean that a retransmission delay incurred will be too large for a small number of collisions.

Hybrids of these CCAs are possible which are more adaptive in nature. Here, the mean retransmission delay would be more heavily penalized whenever the number of collisions exceeded a certain threshold. Moura and Field [37] showed from simulation studies that the BEB performed the least efficiently because it overreacted to repetitive collisions. The retransmission delay computed was too long so that transmission did not occur even when the medium became idle. The BEB also appeared to be sensitive to an increased subscriber population.

The performances of LIB and FMB were approximately equivalent. The former proved slightly better at lower loads and the latter slightly better at higher loads.

The authors then introduce an orderly back-off (OB) algorithm by allowing transmission to proceed in a prescribed sequence whenever traffic exceeds a certain level.

Appendix B

The Effective Data Rates of the Cambridge Ring (40 Bit Circulating Slot)

If the basic data rate = 10 Mbps, then the bandwidth excluding overheads
$$= (16/40) \times 10 \text{ Mbps}$$
$$= 4 \text{ Mbps.}$$

Assume the ring can accommodate three circulating slots only. At any one time, one node may only use one circulating slot. When the slot returns to its source, it is declared empty, but it is unavailable to the source.

There exists an approximate two-slot delay before the source may resume transmission and this may only proceed if the slot is empty. Thus one source may only use one slot in five. And the effective data rate will not exceed
$$(1/5) \times 4 \text{ Mbps} = 0.8 \text{ Mbps.}$$

When the data rate is doubled from 10 to 20 Mbps, the bandwidth excluding overheads is $(16/40) \times 20$ Mbps = 8 Mbps.

The number of slots has also doubled (from 3 to 6) but the two-slot delay still exists. Hence one source may use one in eight packets. Thus the effective data rate
$$= (1/8) \times 8 \text{ Mbps}$$
$$= 1 \text{ Mbps.}$$

Hence, doubling the bandwidth does not double the effective data rate.

It could be argued that as each slot is required to make one complete circulation of the ring, half the bandwidth is squandered on average (from the destination to the source), as this bandwidth is not available to other stations wishing to transmit. Thus, in the above approximations there may be a case for a further reduction in the data rates.

137

The counter-argument rests in the fact that the returning slot is not wasted as it contains useful information (acknowledgements) in the form of response bits (Fig. 9b).

This illustrates the difficulty encountered in successfully modelling such systems as there are many other parameters that may be influential, e.g. node buffer sizes, message delay, message arrival, message length, error rates, and the terminal population. For simplicity none of these have been included in the calculations above, but the reader should be aware of the limited nature of many simulations.

Appendix C
LAN Products and Their Vendors

1. Ring Products
1.1 Cambridge Ring Products

Cambridge Ring

Acorn Computers Ltd
4a Market Hill
Cambridge
CB2 3NJ
UK

Data Ring

Toltec Computer Ltd
Computer Systems
24 Thomson's Lane
Cambridge
CB5 8AQ
UK

Polynet

Logica VTS Ltd
86 Newman Street
London
W1A 4SE
UK

TransRing 2000

Scientific and Electronic Enterprises
   Ltd
3 Young Square
Brucefield South Industrial Park
Livingston
West Lothian
Scotland
UK

Planet

Racal-Milgo Ltd
Landata House
Station Road
Hook
Hampshire
RG27 9JF
UK

1.2 Other Ring Products

SILK

Hasler (GB) Ltd
Commerce Way
Croydon
CR0 4XA
Surrey
UK

Xinet/Xibus

Xionics Ltd
Dumbarton House
68 New Oxford Street
London
W1N 9LA
UK

DOMAIN

Apollo Computer (UK) Ltd
Bulborne House
Gossoms End
Berkhamstead
Hertfordshire
HP4 3LP
UK

Apollo Computer Inc.
19 Alpha Road
Chelmsford
Massachusetts 01824
USA

ODR-1

Syscon Ltd
68 Hills Road
Cambridge
CB2 1LA
UK

Clearway

Real Time Developments Ltd
Lynchford House
Lynchford Lane
Farnborough
Hampshire
GU14 6JA
UK

Multilink

Hawker Siddeley Dynamics
    Engineering Ltd
Bridge Road East
Welwyn Garden City
Hertfordshire
AL7 1LR
UK

Pronet

Proteon Associates Inc.
24 Crescent Street
Waltham
Massachusetts 02154
USA

2. Non-Ring Products

2.1 Single Vendor Supported LANs

Cluster/One

Zynar Ltd
122–123 High Street

Uxbridge
UB8 1JT
UK

Nestar Systems Inc.
Palo Alto
California
USA

HiNet

The Exchange Telegraph Company
    Ltd
73–75 Scrutton Street
London
EC2A 4TA
UK

Modata Ltd
30 St Johns Road
Tunbridge Wells
Kent
TN4 9NT
UK

Digital Microsystems Inc.
1840 Embarcadero
Oakland
California 94606
USA

Omninet

Keen Computers Ltd
Minerva House
Spaniel Row
Nottingham
NG1 6EP
UK

Corvus Systems
2029 O'Toole Avenue
San Jose
California 95131
USA

Z-Net

Zilog(UK) Ltd
Babbage House

Maidenhead
SL6 1DU
Berkshire
UK

Thame Systems Ltd
Thame Park Industrial Estate
Thame
Oxfordshire
OX9 3RS
UK

Zilog Inc.
10460 Bubb Road
Cupertina
California 95014
USA

2.2   Multivendor Supported LANs

Econet

Acorn Computers Ltd
4a Market Hill
Cambridge
CB2 3NJ
UK

Ethernet

Digital Equipment Corp.
Maynard
Massachusetts 01754
USA

Intel Corp.
Santa Clara
California 95051
USA

Xerox Corp.
Stamford
Connecticut 06904
USA

Hyperbus

Tesdata Ltd
Tesdata House
Hatfield Road
Slough

Berkshire
SL1 1QR
UK

Network Systems Corp.
7600 Boone Avenue North
Minneapolis
Minnesota 55428
USA

Net/One

Thame Systems Ltd
Thame Park Industrial Estate
Thame
Oxfordshire
OX9 3RS
UK

Ungermann-Bass Inc.
2560 Mission College Boulevard
Santa Clara
California 95060
USA

2.3   Broadband Systems

LocalNet

Network Technology Ltd
Unit 8 Sutton Park Avenue
Suttons Industrial Park
Reading
Berkshire
RG6 1AZ
UK

Sytek Inc.

1153 Bordeaux Drive
Sunnyvale
California 94086
USA

WangNet

Wang (UK) Ltd
Wang House
100 George Street
London W1
UK

Wang Laboratories Inc.
1 Industrial Avenue
Lowell
Massachusetts 01851
USA

Videodata

Interactive Systems/3M (UK) Ltd
3M House
P.O. Box 1
Bracknell
Berkshire
RG12 1JU
UK

Interactive Systems/3M Corp.
3980 Varsity Drive
Ann Arbor
Michigan 48104
USA

BIS

Philips Data Systems
Electra House
Bergholt Road
Colchester
Essex
CO4 5BE
UK

Philips Data Systems
IPC Paris
France

2.4   High-Speed LANs

Hyperchannel

Tesdata Ltd
Tesdata House
Hatfield Road

Slough
Berkshire
SL1 1QR
UK

Network Systems Corp.
7600 Boone Avenue North
Minneapolis
Minnesota 55428
USA

LCN

Control Data Ltd
Control Data House
179–199 Shaftesbury Avenue
London
WC2H 8AR
UK

Control Data Corp.
Computer Systems Marketing
P.O. Box 0
Minneapolis
Minnesota 55420
USA

Ubits

Amecon Division
Litton Industries
College Park
Maryland
USA

IDX-3000

M/A-Com Linkabit Inc.
3033 Science Park Road
San Diego
California 92121
USA

Appendix D

The Relationship Between the
Bandwidth and Data Rate
of a Channel

(The reader is referred to Tanenbaum [3].)

Nyquist (1924) first formulated the relationship between the maximum data rate of a noiseless channel and its finite bandwidth. Nyquist's theorem states:

the maximum data rate $= 2H \log_2 V$ bps

where $V =$ the number of discrete levels in the signal (i.e. binary $= 2$) and $H =$ bandwidth.

This theorem is applicable where an arbitrary signal has been run through the finite bandwidth noiseless channel which has been subjected to a low pass filter of bandwidth H. Nyquist discovered that this signal could be completely rebuilt by making only $2H$(exact) samples per second. Increasing the rate of sampling is futile as the higher-frequency components have been filtered out.

Shannon extended the work of Nyquist to noisy channels. His work concluded:

maximum no. of bps $= H \log_2(1 + S/N)$

where $S/N =$ signal to noise ratio (signal power to noise power).

If $S/N = 1000$ then for a channel with a bandwidth of 3 kHz, transmission at rates exceeding 30 kbps is not possible, no matter how many signal levels are used or how frequently sampling occurs, that is

$$
\begin{aligned}
\text{maximum no. of bps} &= H \log_2(1 + 1000) \\
&= H \log_2(1001) \\
&= H \times 10 \\
&= 3k \times 10 \\
&= 30 \text{ kbps}
\end{aligned}
$$

143

The reader should note that the formula above merely sets an upper limit on the maximum data rate of a channel. In practice, it is highly unlikely that such utilization of the bandwidth is even approached.

Appendix E

(i) The Allocation of Bandwidth on Broadband LANs

It should be noted that the efforts of IEEE 802 to standardize LANs extends to a standard on how the bandwidth should be divided up for broadband LANs. The origin of this effort was the Electronic Industries Association (EIA) document TR 40.1 and has culminated in its incorporation into IEEE 802 [152].

Simply the standard describes the allocation of the frequency spectrum 5–300 MHz over a single cable. The frequency range 5–108 MHz is reserved for stations transmitting packets on the network which are received by a central retransmit facility (CRF). The CRF shifts (retransmits) the signal by 192.25 MHz and this is received by 'listening' stations between the frequencies 180 and 216 MHz. Inbound and outbound signals to and from the CRF are prevented from interfering with each other by the allocation of an unused guardband (108–162 MHz). Furthermore, television transmission is reserved for the frequency range 180–216 MHz and 24–60 MHz is reserved for 6 MHz channels only.

It should be noted that none of the LAN broadband products outlined in the book conform exactly to this proposed standard. Videodata is the closest as it utilizes the same frequency shift. It also uses the approximate bandwidths 5–11 MHz and 162–168 MHz for audio transmit and receive.

LocalNet diverges from the proposed standard a little more as the frequency shift used is 156.25 MHz. The CRFs receive frequencies of 40–70 MHz and are occupied by System 40 which encroaches on the 24–60 MHz range reserved for 6 MHz channels.

WangNet is incompatible with other broadband products and the proposed standard, as it is a dual-cable system where the bandwidth is not split for transmission and reception, i.e. no frequency shift is involved, stations transmit at a particular frequency on one of the cables, and reception occurs at the same frequency on the other cable.

(ii) The Effect of Using CSMA-CD on a Baseband LAN, a Single-Cable Broadband LAN, and a Dual-Cable Broadband LAN

In the three cases examined, the worst possible cases as regards the effect of CSMA-CD are presented.

It will be shown that for three topologically equivalent systems (a simple bus), the time to detect a collision is twice for broadband systems than for baseband systems. The CRF and the 'loop', for the single- and dual-cable broadband systems respectively, are assumed to be at one end of the bus.

For a baseband system, the worst possible case for the time to detect a collision occurs when Station A at one extreme end of the bus transmits and just before the signal reaches the other end of the bus, Station B positioned there detects the carrier as idle and also begins transmitting. A collision results and this will travel in the opposite direction back to the source of the original transmission, i.e. Station A. Thus the time for Station A to detect a collision can be approximated to the time it takes for the signal to propagate from one end of the bus to the other (t) plus the corresponding time for the collision to propagate to the station A (t). Hence, the time to detect a collision on a baseband LAN cannot exceed the time for the signal to propagate twice the length of the bus ($2t$).

For a single-cable broadband system where the bandwidth is divided into transmit (F1) and receive halves (F2), the worst time to detect a collision occurs when Stations A and B are positioned at the same end of the bus but at the opposite end to the CRF. If Station A transmits a message, the signal propagates to the CRF where it is 'shifted' and retransmitted (F2) back down to the bus ($2t$). Just before the shifted signal (F2) reaches Station B, the receive circuitry will discover that the cable is passive at that particular frequency channel and begin transmitting in the unshifted frequency range (F1). The signal from Station B collides with the signal from Station A at F1 and this propagates to the CRF which in turn shifts the garbled signal to F2 and this is received by Station A which is then aware of the occurrence of a collision. Here, the collision has travelled twice the length of the bus before the collision is actually detected by the source resulting in a further time of $2t$ on a

146

broadband bus. Thus, the worst case for collision detection occurs when two stations are attempting to transmit and they are both situated right at the opposite end to the CRF. The contention interval approximates to four times the time for a signal to propagate one length of the bus ($4t$).

A dual-cable broadband LAN also presents a worst case contention period of four times the time for a signal to propagate the length of the bus. The description of this LAN as dual-cable results in a slight confusion. It is, in reality, one length of cable which doubles back (loops) on itself. Hence, the same topological assumption as used for the other two LANs in this appendix necessitates twice the length of cable in this case. Here, the 'loop' is topologically equivalent to the CRF. In this LAN, the bandwidth is not divided into transmit and receive halves and thus the contention interval is double that for a baseband system merely because the cable length is twice as long. The dual cable nature is necessitated because of the monodirectional nature of the transmitters and receivers used. Each station is attached to what appears as two different pieces of cable but, in reality, this is the attachment of the transmitter and receiver to two different points on the same cable.

It should be emphasized, however, that the two cases for the single-cable and the dual-cable broadband LANs outlined here are the worst within the assumptions made. To some degree, this can be overcome by attention being given to the design of the network, and the optimal placement of the CRF in the middle of the bus topology considered in the above examples would result in a contention window of time $2t$ and not $4t$ if the CRF were placed at one end of the bus.

Appendix F
An Update on the Work of IEEE 802

After some considerable initial effort, IEEE 802 defined a LAN as follows:

A local area network is distinguished from other types of data networks in that communications is usually confined to a moderate sized geographic area such as a single office building, a warehouse, or a campus, and can depend on a physical communications channel of moderate to high data rate which has a consistently low error rate.

A comparison of some of the definitions offered in Chapter 1 reveals some differences. In the IEEE 802 definition, there has been no attempt to quantify data rates, e.g. compare the definition offered by Tanenbaum [3]. There is no reference to single organizational proprietorship [3,9] nor that a LAN should contain elements of switching technology [1]. Furthermore, the locality of the LAN is merely referred to as a 'moderate sized geographic area'.

The problems presented in LAN definition have already been observed, but IEEE 802 produced some other definitions as a common platform for further discussion. These additional definitions included coexistence (the non- interference of two stations coexisting on a medium), communication (two stations sharing a common set of rules that enables message exchange), and determinism (the modelling of a system as a 'deterministic finite state machine').

The intention of IEEE 802 was that the use of these definitions and the ISO OSI-7 layered model would serve as a common point of reference and facilitate the process of LAN standardization, but this has not proved to be the case.

IEEE 802 has had its critics. It has been considered that the committee has compromised by trying to adopt a standard (Draft B) that contained CSMA-CD as well as a token passing scheme. The incompatible nature of these two techniques necessitates expensive software to bridge this. However, this proposal was rejected as two-thirds of the membership either abstained or requested modifications. This unusual occurrence (as regards standards committees) has been interpreted as a weakness in Project 802 committee leadership.

However, the outcome was the specification of a new standard defining separate access methods for each LAN medium. This would make twisted pair based LANs incompatible with coaxial or lightwave based systems [153]. As the nature of the transmission media has figured prominently in the work of the IEEE 802, its incorporation as the lowest level (Layer 0) into the ISO OSI reference model has thus been proposed [109].

In defence, Project 802 consider their situation to be unique. First, it is an attempt to establish standards in advance of the market, as without them the market would never realize its full potential. Secondly, many institutions (commercial and academic) have participated to a significant degree. Thirdly, its scope is unrivalled as it provides not only a model but specifies the interface and the protocol for logical link control (LLC), access techniques, encoding techniques, and physical media. Furthermore, the committee argue that the notion that one LAN solution exists is fallacious [154].

The result of the committee's work is a comprehensive specification (Draft C) that possesses CSMA-CD, a token ring, and a token bus subsection. The draft embraced Ethernet supporting 48 bit addressing, the Manchester encoding technique, and permitting the 46 byte minimum frame of Ethernet to be supported [155]. The token passing subsections, previously incomplete, now subscribe to a networking scheme provided almost wholly by IBM. This was a response to severe criticism of Draft B which had not included sufficient detail on token passing. The token ring will standardize a shielded twisted pair medium at transmission rates of 1 and 4 Mbps and a coaxial cable medium at 4 and 10 Mbps. Token bus is supported on both single and multichannel coaxial cable (broadband), the latter being CATV-compatible at transmission rates of 1, 5, 10, and 20 Mbps.

The committee's endeavours have resulted in a tree-like standard that concentrates on the physical and data link layers of the ISO reference model. A common logical link control (LLC) provides an unconnected datagram-like service and a fully connected service similar to HDLC. Below the LLC exist three major branches: CSMA-CD bus, token bus, and token ring.

It thus appears that IEEE 802 has abandoned its hope for a media-independent access technique and that a move is under way to associate a particular medium with each access method [156]. Furthermore, one of the original design objectives was to maintain compatibility with other standards bodies, the most notable being the ISO and the OSI reference model [156,157].

In terms of the media access, it is problematic where channel access protocols should be placed in the OSI reference model, which does not address this issue at all [158]. The uncertainty is highlighted in broadcast networks where a protocol is required to prevent channel overload. Here, as each host receives every packet no routing decisions have to be made. Thus, the channel access protocol could be placed in the data link layers as it is concerned with getting packets from one machine to the next. Alternatively, it could be placed at the network layer since it also concerns getting packets from the source host to the destination host. Another argument for the network layer is that the main task of the access protocol is to prevent channel congestion and this is specifically a network layer function.

IEEE 802 have decided to include media access as part of the data link layer. In fact, this layer consists of two sublayers: data link and media access control. The layer is referred to as the DLMAC layer [157].

In addition to the four main subcommittees which are concerned with physical level protocols, link level protocols, CSMA-CD, and token passing, two other subcommittees have recently been included under Project 802.

The first new subcommittee is called the 'High Level Interface' subcommittee. The aims of this particular subcommittee are to consider higher-level aspects of LANs such as network management, internetworking, and addressing [159].

The second new subcommittee is concerned with 'Metropolitan Networks' [160]. It is this subcommittee which no longer focuses on just LANs, but is also considering networks over greater distances such as 50 km. Issues under consideration here include the employment of different network technologies and protocols, e.g. circuit switching technology and TDM reservation.

Appendix G

European Computers Manufacturers Association (ECMA) Standards

Among some of the 18 companies who have recently announced their intention to use ECMA standards are ICL, CII-Honeywell Bull, Hewlett Packard, ITL, Logica VTS, LM Ericsson, Mitel Corporation, NTL, Olivetti, Siemens, Ungermann-Bass, 3Com, and the Three Rivers Corporation [161].

ECMA's efforts in standardizing LANs go further than the IEEE. Apart from addressing specification for the media, physical layer, and the datalink layer, a transport protocol is also included. The intervening network layer was not specified but it was noted that X.25 could perform some interim function. A general purpose transport layer protocol was considered important as this will allow multivendor compatibilty and intercommunication between different LANs. An important point to note is that the transport layer specification of ECMA is consistent with that of the ISO (TC 97/SG 16). A broadband standard is under current consideration.

However, any standards support from companies that do not include IBM and Wang must cast doubt on this effort [162].

Appendix H

Some Indications on IBM's LAN Offering

Although IBM have not officially announced or launched any LAN product as yet [163] (apart from the Series/1 ring and IBM 8100 loop which employed register insertion and polling techniques respectively), there are many signs to indicate that the company is likely to offer a baseband LAN utilizing a single token access protocol. It is in this area that IBM have been making active and significant contributions to IEEE 802 and the following outlines some of the details that have emerged.

Hardware and Configuration

It appears that IBM consider that the needs of the office of the future may be satisfied by a 1–4 Mbps baseband, single token passing LAN where nodes are interconnected by twisted pair copper wires forming a star-ring topology. The interconnection of subnetworks via bridges enables the construction of a larger local network. Here a bridge is a high-speed digital switch capable of buffering frames, transmission speed conversion, and transparent logical routing.

Modus Operandi

On each ring, one station acts as an active token monitor whilst others monitor passively. In the event of a malfunction, any one of the passive monitors can assume the role of an active monitor. Packet transmission occurs in frames of variable length after a station has seized the token. The header and the trailer fields include start and ending delimiters, source and destination addresses, a 'free' or 'busy' token bit, and a frame check sequence (FCS). Other fields exist to facilitate flexibility and fault detection, viz. an address recognized indicator bit, an error detected indicator bit, and a priority bit.

A station sets the address recognized bit and logs a possible duplicate address if it detects that its address has already been recognized. All stations check the FCS and the first station detecting an error sets the error detected indicator for purposes of fault localization.

Applications which demand more timely ring access are accommodated by the use of a priority mode, where the lowest priority is assigned to data or non-conversational digitized voice. At the next level, an asynchronous priority is assigned for bridge access to rings to reduce congestion. The real-time servicing requirements of conversational voice and facsimile applications are assigned to a synchronous higher priority.

The integration of synchronous and asynchronous traffic necessitates a mechanism that will interrupt the normal flow of asynchronous data traffic. A synchronous bandwidth manager node can prevent a free token from being issued by setting a flag in a physical control field of a frame. Prior to releasing a token, a node must check the state of this flag. If the flag is set, the bandwidth is made available to synchronous traffic by deferring asynchronous traffic.

The synchronous bandwidth manager can also interrupt asynchronous traffic by setting the interrupt flag on the next frame that passes the controller node. On average, the suspension of asynchronous traffic and the subsequent initiation of synchronous traffic requires one frame time.

Error detection and recovery mechanisms

Essential to the reliable operation of the LAN is the token monitor. This station is responsible for proper token operation and rapid recovery from token or noise errors. Additional diagnostics determine whether one particular station is endangering ring operation. Subsequent removal of a ring segment or a station through bypass logic and closing a bypass switch may result.

The occurrence of a lost token, e.g. on ring initialization or a noise disturbance, is detected by the monitor using a time-out with a period longer than the longest frame permitted to traverse the ring. Removal of all residual data and free token generation then ensues.

To prevent the indefinite circulation of busy tokens, e.g. the failure of a station before the removal of its token or a noise altering a free token to a busy one, a monitor count bit is used. (Compare this to the monitor bit on the circulating slots, which are set by the monitor station on the Cambridge Ring.) This bit is set when a busy token passes the monitor station. If the busy token recirculates then the monitor count bit will indicate that the source has failed to remove its token. Consequently, the monitor will remove this erroneous token and generate a free one. In this respect, the Cambridge Ring could thus be considered as a case of multiple tokens where only fixed length packets can be transmitted. However, the existence of multiple tokens on a possible IBM LAN is an error condition. This situation could be created by noise or the disruption and subsequent loss when two stations transmit concurrently.

The passive monitors use a free token time-out with different periods for each station to determine the loss of the active monitor. The assumption of an active role by a passive monitor is achieved by the generation of a busy token and a monitor active signal in the data field. Contention between stations is prevented by the passive monitor sending a signal until it receives one from a station with a greater source address, which it concedes to, or an equal address, in which case it assumes the role of the new active monitor station.

Fault Detection and Isolation

The claim made here is that fault detection and isolation are facilitated by the connection of distributed office links to centralized wiring concentrators positioned in wire cabinets. (This results in the star-ring topology.) Here, a network lobe may be bypassed by using switching elements within each wiring concentrator. Implementation of the lobe bypass may be via manual or automatic switches. Alternatively, this may be remotely effected by the receipt of the appropriate network management commands.

Faulty wiring, concentrators or cable severance necessitates reconfiguration and this is facilitated by a secondary ring, running parallel to the primary ring, on which signal propagation may occur in the opposite direction. Re-routing the primary transmission path back along the alternate ring at both wiring concentrators immediately adjacent to the detected fault allows the fault to be isolated.

Rationale

The design goals of IBM's possible LAN offering have included the provision of network reliability and flexibility. These goals should be placed in the context of geographically dispersed office complexes which interconnect large numbers of terminals and workstations and integrate data, voice, and facsimile applications.

In this respect, IBM consider that a token passing protocol allows the priorization of demand access to the network and, consequently, the accommodation of real-time applications. Furthermore, it is asserted that the primary advantage of the single token strategy is its simplicity, as regards the design of a robust priority scheme and error recovery, combined with an efficiency comparable to a multiple token scheme.

IBM regard the token passing architecture as corresponding to the physical layer of the ISO OSI-7 layered model. Furthermore, it is regarded that the protocols within SNA can be used over LANs and any data link control station can be interfaced without modification, allowing the accommodation of different vendor's architectures.

Finally, the company maintain that there is no commitment to a particular product offering, but a 4 Mbps voice/data network has been implemented at IBM, Zurich, using Series/1s computers with over 100 stations and approximately 5 km of cable [164]. Some observers of IBM's option for a baseband token passing scheme have interpreted this as a short-term measure, as the software intensity of the approach permits upgradability towards more advanced networking technologies utilizing media like coaxial cable, fibre optics, and microwave, but these are not anticipated before 1984 or 1985 [165].

Notes

Introduction

1. When compared with the best speed currently available on packet switched networks—48 kbps—or the conventional telephone network— 9.6 kbps—LAN data rates are very impressive.

Chapter 1

2. Tanenbaum's use of the term 'diameter' is questionable in that LANs need not connote a circular structure.

3. The reader should note that some products offered by their vendors as LANs neither possess data rates which are greater than 1 Mbps nor do some contain elements of switching, whilst simultaneously satisfying the remaining two criteria.

4. It must be noted that the aspect of sole proprietorship with reference to LANs is something which is now being debated. Previously, most—if not all —definitions of LANs either explicitly or implicitly considered sole proprietorship to be a central aspect of LANs. Now, however, this is less clear. A number of individuals have made reference to LANs being installed in office blocks. In this case one LAN may be used and owned by a number of different organizations. Quite often these multiproprietorship LANs are discussed for use in energy management systems, video systems, etc., as well as the more common data and text systems.

Chapter 2

5. No attempt will be made to define office automation or distributed processing here, but it is recognized that there is a strong correlation between these trends and microprocessor development. In all likelihood, the latter has been the initiating factor in the co-development of office automation and distributed processing.

6. A report from International Resource Management has stated 'the market for local networks and short range communication equipment is expected to grow to a $3.2 billion industry by 1990' [13].

7. The methods employed by office information systems and to which

particular strata of the organization they are directed are important issues but are beyond the scope of this book.

Chapter 3

8. The reader's attention is drawn once again to the geographical scope of LANs. Compare and contrast Cotton's [11] notion of the geographical locality with some of the definitions in the first section. It should be noted that some LAN products are more concerned with the same room, rather than the same building or campus.

9. Some LANs broadcast to all other stations thus supplying full logical interconnections without full physical interconnection. This will be considered in greater detail when topologies are examined.

10. LAN-WAN interconnection presents problems as well as benefits as their protocols must be made compatible at some point. This will be discussed in Part II of the book.

11. There are problems however, e.g. the revision of documents created on different vendor's equipment.

Chapter 4

12. It should be borne in mind that the vendor and his reputation should play an important role in an evaluation of LAN products. A potential implementor may be prepared to trade off a degree less of sophistication for the serviceability and the maintainability of the supplier's package.

13. For instance, it is more usual to associate a bus topology with a contention control strategy and a ring with daisy chain control, but contention rings and bus topologies with daisy chain ring control strategy are possible [7]. An example of the former includes the LAN implemented at the Computer Science Laboratory at MIT and an example of the latter is the UNIBUS architecture of DEC.

14. Here again, the problem of defining the geographical scope of the LAN surfaces. However, Weitzman [24] actually asserts that a distinction between the classes of systems he recognizes can be significantly related to the level of geographical dispersion:

> '... a shared memory-based multiminicomputer system is usually contained in one or two adjacent racks, whereas a bus or looped-based system may be distributed within a single structure. A hierarchical system can be dispersed between several plants or buildings, whereas a packet or circuit switched system may have one or more minicomputers located on the west coast of the US and others on the east coast or even in Europe.'

Chapter 5

15. The debate is also geographically polarized between the USA, and Great Britain and Europe. Contention (bus) LANs predominate in the USA because of the organizations responsible for the Ethernet development, namely Xerox, DEC, and Intel. In Britain and Europe, a great deal of research is being invested in rings, but this has not received the same scale of commercial backing as the Ethernet.

16. A review of some of the products will be featured in Part II of this book.

17. The Cambridge Ring uses a four-wire (two signal paths) modulation scheme because this was considered appropriate for a pair of twisted wires. A zero is signified by a change on one of the pairs and a one is signified by a change on both pairs, at each clock instant. In contrast with phase modulation there is no ambiguity concerning the start of the digit.

18. Ring hardware was originally constructed using TTL technology. A repeater and a station unit contain 12 and 66 TTL packages respectively, but these are being replaced by a pair of uncommitted logic array (ULA) chips, where the circuit of the repeater and the station unit is divided between them. The shift registers for reception and transmission would be external to the chips, giving flexibility in the choice of packet length. This would also facilitate the provision of a parallel data connection to the access box, along with the usual serial connection to the ring.

19. In contrast, the register insertion scheme experiences the largest delays around the ring, but the initial delay before the register is inserted is small.

20. This results in the segmented topology referred to in Section 4.2.2.

21. The interface was responsible for data serializing (deserializing) by the station computing and checking the cyclic redundancy checksums (CRCs) and the acceptance of those packets addressed to the station it serves. The controller was responsible for retransmission of colliding or unacknowledged packets.

22. The SERC has recently announced its intentions regarding an evaluation of the Cambridge Ring and the Ethernet [32].

23. The design problems which arise in the contention bus and which do not arise in the ring are mainly concerned with the nature of the cable transceiver. Some of these points are outlined below, but the diligence in its design will affect the overall dependability and performance of the network.

Basically, the transceiver must present a high impedance to the bus except during its own transmission, otherwise this may interfere with a transmission from another transceiver. The ability to detect collisions also impacts upon the encoding scheme used for the transmissions. The transceiver must also be capable of tolerating the ground potential differences at various hosts on the network. This necessitates the isolation of transceiver and host circuitry to prevent erroneous current flows interfering with signals on the cable [7].

Transformer, optical, and capacitive techniques are possible but the former was selected for the Ethernet because it was the most cost competitive compared to optical techniques and had better common mode rejection than the capacitive isolation method [33].

24. Compare the claims of Shoch and Hupp that the Ethernet's adaptive randomization strategy minimizes delay under light loads, yet remains stable under heavy loads [166].

Chapter 6

25. SSP messages are combined to transfer character files around the network and at each end of the communication the byte stream appears as a standard file.

26. The exact function of the extra two bits on a 40 bit circulating slot is uncertain, but it is possible that they could be used by higher-level protocols.

27. Twisted pair and fibre optic versions will also be developed utilizing Racal Milgo's own microelectronic technology.

28. Compare the Cambridge Ring, in which the packet is required to return to its source although acknowledgments are 'piggy backed'.

29. Xionics are still refining the store-and-forward features necessary for speech. It has been successful in compressing digitized speech, as one minute of speech will produce 190 kbytes of data under those conditions [57].

30. In actuality, the DMA channel is common to the disk and the network enabling data transfer rates to approach the full memory bandwidth. If network and disk transfer coincide, one device is required to make an additional revolution. The manufacturers claim that the effect of this interference on performance is negligible.

31. Compare ODR-1 with the Cambridge Ring which is also an active ring. If a repeater fails on the Cambridge Ring, the system is completely disabled until fault detection and correction.

32. The present bandwidth (500 kHz) is low in relation to the bandwidths that fibre optics can support. Corning have manufactured a waveguide using a vapour phase oxidation doped deposited silica process which exhibited a test bandwidth exceeding 3 GHz/km [60].

33. The transporter is designed for direct memory access (DMA) of the host computer by a 24 bit memory address and in which a gate array controls the transporter/host interface. This logic, which does not need to buffer any data, also controls the RS422 driver and receiver circuitry—the network transceiver. A Motorola MC6854 Advanced Data Link Controller (ADLC) provides the network interface to the carrier and implements data link control functions such as bit serialization, the generation of the cyclic redundancy checksum, packet framing, and carrier sensing. The gate array and the ADLC are both coordinated by a Motorola MC6801 microprocessor (with 2k ROM and 128k RAM) and this is responsible for the conversion and transfer of data and control information between the host and the network.

34. The System 8000 network interface board is a Z8001 based communications processor. It possesses 128 kbytes of RAM, 32 kbytes PROM and provides two high-speed (800 kbps) serial ports.

35. UNET provides three modes of communication for the user: virtual terminal, file transfer, and mail system.

36. Acorn give an example of 20 users attempting to load their files from disk. From typing the command to completion, it takes about 1 second to load a 1k file from disk. Thus, the last user will have to wait 19 seconds! However, the manufacturers claim that the usual network access would not occur simultaneously and this will reduce the wait time.

37. In an effort to make Ethernet a *de facto* standard, licences were sold cheaply to any company wishing to manufacture Ethernet compatible hardware, e.g. 3COM Corporation and Interlan Inc., in the USA, and Sension Scientific and Geac Computers Ltd, in the UK, amongst many others.

38. At the time, the other was considered to be an IBM standard.

39. The host interfaces are based on Intel 8086 16 bit microprocessors and sell for about $10000. IBM data channel, DEC Unibus, and Intel Multibus Interfaces are available. In System 20, terminal interface units are Zilog Z80 8 bit microprocessor based, operate at 128 kbps, and cost $1100.

40. In System 20, the 120 channels each have a bandwidth of 300 kHz and are contained in two 36 MHz bands. The 70–106 MHz band is used for data transmission from any packet communication unit (PCU) to the broadband translator (central retransmission facility). This converts the low band to a high band (226–262 MHz) for retransmission to the receive section of each PCU.

41. Compare WangNet with LocalNet. The latter possesses a single coaxial cable but source transmission and message reception occupy different parts of the total bandwidth.

42. Model 5991 possesses transmitter and receiver bandwidths of 6 MHz and 4 MHz respectively.

43. Common to most broadband LANs is the division of the bandwidth into a transmission half and a reception half. In Videodata, the Data Remodulator performs this function and this is equivalent to the central retransmission facility (CRF) on LocalNet. The loop on WangNet provides the exception.

44. Two dedicated frequency channels are required because of the monodirectional nature of CATV components, e.g. taps, splitters, and amplifiers.

45. The forward channel transmits data received on the reverse channel passing through a head end of a frequency shift. This is provided by some centralized function and is common to most broadband systems. The reverse channel is time division multiplexed as dictated by the logical ring access procedure (token passing).

46. Compare Hyperchannel with Ethernet, where all stations have equal status.

Chapter 8

47. A LAN report entitled 'Intra-Company Networks: Broadband vs. Baseband—the key issues' from Strategic Inc. reached a different conclusion. The report contends that the costs of broadband LANs are competitive even for smaller applications and in many practical configurations are less expensive than an equivalent Ethernet system [106].

48. The reader should be aware of the many ways that systems could be distributed over a LAN and how each exploits the services that a particular subnetwork offers. Tanenbaum [3] summarizes these into five models for distributing computations: (1) a hierarchical model, (2) a CPU cache model, (3) a user server model, (4) the pool processor model,

and (5) the data flow model—which is one of the architectures considered in the 'Fifth Generation Project'. The latter represents the most extreme form of distribution where processor cooperation takes place in executing a single program.

For a good discussion of the issues involved in the 'Fifth Generation Project' the reader's attention is directed to reference [114]. References [115] and [116] compare in detail two alternatives to the data flow model. These are the control flow and the reduction models. A treatment of these models is beyond the scope of this text.

Chapter 9

49. This statement may be debated by some who consider Datapoint's ARC as a LAN. There have been some 3000 sales of ARC worldwide. Yet ARC is not, in the strictest sense, a LAN but rather a local minicomputer network for Datapoint equipment; in fact, it was never advertised as a LAN, only a local network. It is only relatively recently that ARC has been described as a LAN—mostly by the Datapoint sales force. More on this later.

50. See Tables 1 and 2 in Chapter 1.

51. Given the enormous interest which has been shown to exist in LANs, plus the general lack of specific knowledge on LANs, it is not too surprising that the manufacturers supplying LCNs have tended to market them as LANs.

52. See Mintzberg [129] for a good treatment on the issue of centralization and its relationship with bureaucratization (pp. 195–8).

Chapter 10

53. For an excellent treatment on implementation research see the writings of Michael Ginzberg at New York University.

54. A detailed description of the actual participation and socio-technical system process is beyond the scope of this book. It has been written up in the past and appears in various books and articles. Those readers who wish to know more about the process are referred [141], [147], and [148].

55. It should be noted that some think of the facilitator as an individual who knows about both the technology and the social arrangements. Not all agree that this is a necessary requirement of a facilitator, however.

56. Quite often determining precisely who 'all affected users' are will not be easy. However, Klein and Hirschheim [149] have proposed an approach based on role playing and hermeneutics, which could be invaluable in user determination.

References

1. Freeman, H.A. and Thurber, K.J., 'Updated bibliography on local computer networks', *Compt. Arch. News*, **8**, April 1980, 20–28.
2. Thurber, K.J. and Freeman, H.A., 'Architecture considerations for local area computer networks', *Proceedings of the First International Conference on Distributed Computing Systems*, October 1979, 131–142.
3. Tanenbaum, A.S., *Computer Networks*, Prentice-Hall, 1981, Chap.7.
4. Edhart, J.L., 'Understanding local area networks', *Seybold Report on Word Processing*, **4**, no.6, June 1981.
5. Farber, D.J. and Larson, K.C., 'The system architecture of the distributed computer system—the communication system', *Symposium on Computer Networks*, Polytechnic Institute of Brooklyn, Brooklyn, New York, April 1972.
6. Metcalfe, R.M. and Boggs, D.R., 'Ethernet: distributed packet switching for local computer networks', *Commun.ACM*, **19**, 1976, 395.
7. Clark, D.D., Pogran, K.T. and Reed, D.P., 'An introduction to local area networks', *Proc.IEEE*, **66**, no.11, November 1978, 1497–1517.
8. Wilkes, M.V., 'The impact of wideband communication systems on distributed computing', Paper presented at *1st International Conference on Distributed Computing Systems*, Huntsville, Alabama, 1–4 October 1979.
9. Cotton, I.W. (ed.), *Local Area Networking*, Report of a Workshop held at the National Bureau of Standards, Gaithersburg, Maryland, 22–23 August 1977.
10. McQuillan, J.M., 'Local network technology and the lessons of history', *Computer Networks*, **4**, 1980, 235–238.
11. Cotton, I.W., 'Techniques for local area networks', *Computer Networks*, **4**, 1980, 197–208.
12. Kingsmill, A., 'Office automation—4, Bringing communication services to the office of the future', *Computer Weekly*, no. 726, 18 June 1981, 29.
13. Grosch, H., 'Ethernet—local approach to shared standards', *Computing*, 13 November 1980.
14. Joyce, C.C., 'Communications network transfer information inside and out', *Word Processing and Information Systems*, June 1981, 30.

15. Kelland, G., 'Office automation—1, How an organisation can move into the future by using a standard networking system', *Computer Weekly*, no.726, 18 June 1981, 26.

16. Spratt, E.B., 'Operational experience with a Cambridge Ring local area network in a university environment', *IFIP WG 6.4 International Workshop on Local Area Networks*, Zurich, August 1980.

17. Dallas, I.N., 'Providing and managing a local network service', *Proceedings of NETWORKSHOP 6*, April 1980.

18. Wilkes, M.V. and Wheeler, D.J., 'The Cambridge Digital Communication Ring', *Local Area Communication Networks Symposium*, MITRE Corp. and National Bureau of Standards, Boston, May 1979.

19. Saltzer, J.H. and Pogran, K.T., 'A star-shaped ring network with high maintainability', *Computer Networks*, 4, 1980, 239–244.

20. Whitely, J., 'Network strategy', *Systems International*, May 1981, 21.

21. Green, R., 'Networks', *Computer Talk*, 24 June 1981, 10.

22. Herbert, A., 'The user interface to the Cambridge Model Distributed System', *Paper presented at the Second International Conference on Distributed Computing Systems*, Versailles, 6–10 April 1981.

23. Wood, A., 'Hobbyists pastime will become the market of the 80's', *Computer Weekly*, 5 March 1981.

24. Hopper, A., 'The Cambridge Ring—a local network', in *Advanced Techniques for Microprocessor Systems*, ed. F.K. Hanna, Peter Peregrinus, 1980.

25. Weitzman, C., *Distributed Micro/Minicomputer Systems: Structure, Implementation and Application*, Prentice-Hall, 1980.

26. Miller, K.C. and Thompson, D.M., 'Making a case for token passing in local networks', *Data Communications*, March 1982, 79–88.

27. Popek, G.J., 'Notes on distributed systems of microprocessors', *Proceedings of Microcomputer System Design*, Course Notes, ed. M.J. Flynn, N.R. Harns and D.P. McCarthy, Trinity College, University of Dublin, June 1981, 287.

28. *Cambridge Digital Communication Ring*, Computer Laboratory, Cambridge University, UK, 19 October 1979.

29. *Xerox Ethernet Communication Systems*, Product Information Bulletin.

30. *The Ethernet—A Local Area Network*, Data Link Layer and Physical Layer Specifications, Version 1.0, 30 September 1980.

31. Hindin, H.J., 'Ethernet is up to date but without surprises; local net concept has 10 Mbps data rate', *Electronics*, 23 October 1980, 42.

32. Shaw, C., 'SERC to evaluate Ethernet network', *Computing*, 9, no.47, 19 November 1981.

33. Shoch, J.F., Dalal, Y.K., Redell, D.D. and Crane, R.C., 'Evolution of the Ethernet local computer network', *Computer*, August 1982, 10–27.

34. Mok, A.K. and Ward, S.A., 'Distributed broadcast channel access', *Computer Networks*, 3, 5 November 1979, 327–335.

35. Shoch, J.F., 'A brief note on performance of an Ethernet system under high load', *Computer Networks*, **14**, no.4, September 1980, 187.

36. Blair, G.S. and Shepherd, D., 'A performance comparison of Ethernet and the Cambridge Digital Communication Ring', *Computer Networks*, **6**, 1982, 105–113.

37. Moura, A. and Field, J., 'Collision-control algorithms in carrier-sense multiple-access (collision-detection) networks', *Computer Communications*, **4**, no. 1, February 1981, 10–18.

38. Hopper, A., *'Local area computer communications network'*, Ph.D. Dissertation, University of Cambridge, Computer Lab., Tech. Rep. 7, April 1978.

39. Leslie, I.M., Banerjee, R., and Love, S.J., 'Organization of voice communication on the Cambridge Ring', in *Local Networks and Distributed Office Systems*, Online Publications, 1981, 465–473.

40. *The Cambridge Ring*, Acorn Computers Ltd, Cambridge.

41. *TOLTEC's Cambridge Data Ring*, Toltec Computer Ltd, Cambridge.

42. Corfield, P., 'The missing link', *Systems International*, March 1981, 47.

43. *Polynet Outline Description*, Polynet Marketing, Logica VTS Ltd, London.

44. *Polynet*, DMA Interface Unit, Logica VTS Ltd, London.

45. *Polynet Components Description and Price List*, Logica VTS Ltd, London.

46. 'Logica—Polynet for 10 universities', *Computer Weekly*, no.781, February 1981.

47. *TransRing Local Area Network 2000 Series*, Scientific and Electronic Enterprises Ltd, Scotland.

48. *TransRing 2000 Terminal Concentrator*, Scientific and Electronic Enterprises Ltd, Scotland.

49. Kennett, D., 'Third Cambridge Ring product launched', *Computer Weekly*, no.755, 30 April 1981.

50. *PLANET—Private Local Area Network*, Racal-Milgo.

51. Kennett, D., 'Racal in network bid', *Computer Weekly*, 15 April 1982, 2.

52. 'Racal leaps into the local area networks', *Computing*, 18 June 1981, 1.

53. *SILK—A Second Generation Local Area Network*, Hasler (GB) Ltd.

54. Schultze, E., 'Simulation of the traffic on the SILK-loop', *Hasler Review*, **12**, no.3/4.

55. Braun, F.G., Hafner, E.R., and Schultze, E., 'System and traffic aspects in SILK: System for Integrated Local Communications', *National Telecommunications Conference*, 30 November-4 December 1980, 65.1.1–65.1.6.

56. *XIBUS/XINET—A Brief Introduction*, Xionics Ltd, London.

57. Connor, S., 'Voices supplant keyboards', *Computing*, 4 March 1982, 19.

58. *Apollo Domain Architecture*, Apollo Computer Inc., August 1981.

59. *Syscon ODR-1 Specification A*, Syscon Systems Consultancy, Cambridge.

60. Parratt, E., 'Broadband, fibres and satellites', *Systems International*, June 1981, 47–50.

61. *Clearway*, Real-Time Developments Ltd.

62. Kennett, D., 'Cheap local net has edge on faster systems', *Computer Weekly*, 21 January 1982, 10.

63. Frank, R.A., 'Another local network surfaces', *Datamation*, November 1981, 89.

64. Local Microcomputer Network System and Back-end Storage Network, *Cluster/One, Model A*, Zynar Ltd, Uxbridge.

65. Crook, C., 'Network Philosophy', *Systems International*, August 1981, 23.

66. 'NCC's Apple net includes viewdata', *Computing*, 10 September 1981.

67. *HiNet*, Modata Digital Microsystems, Tunbridge Wells.

68. *Omninet—Technical Overview*, Keen Computers, Nottingham.

69. Johnston, R., '64-micro network unit', *Computer Weekly*, no.760, 4 June 1981.

70. Estrin, J. and Carrico, W., 'Local network enlists Z80's for distributed processing', *Electronics*, no.760, 10 February 1981.

71. *MCZ-2 and Z-Net*, System Overview, Zilog Inc.

72. *Your Gateway to the Future*, Z-Net product description, Zilog Inc.

73. Marshall, M., 'Z-Net allows easy add ons', *Electronics*, 8 May 1980, 40.

74. *Z-Net II Communications Package for System 8000*, Press Information, Zilog, Exxon Computer Systems.

75. Hauser, H.M., *Technical Specification of the Econet*, Acorn Computers Ltd, Cambridge.

76. *The Acorn Econet*, Acorn Computers Ltd, Cambridge.

77. 'Acorn favours Ethernet type of architecture instead of ring main', *Computing*, **8**, no.46, 13 November 1980.

78. *3COM Ethernet Products*, Price List, Sintrom Group, Berkshire, UK.

79. *Ethernet Transmission Medium*, Price List, Sintrom Group, Berkshire, UK.

80. *Courier: The Remote Procedure Call Protocol*, Xerox System Integration Standard, XSIS 038112, December 1981.

81. *Hyperbus, Preliminary Product Descriptions*, Network Systems Corporation, April 1982.

82. USA Report, 'System grows from network', *Systems International*, May 1982, 59.

83. Whitely, J., 'Soft net', *Systems International*, April 1981.

84. Bass, C., Kennedy, J.S., and Davidson, J.M., 'Local network gives new flexibility to distributed processing', *Electronics*, 25 September 1980, 114.

85. *Net/One—The Local Network for Multivendor Distributed Processing*, Ungermann-Bass, Inc.
86. Davis, R., *The Networking Controversy*, Thame Systems Ltd, December 1981.
87. Dineson, M.A., 'Broadband local networks enhance communication design', *Electrical Design News*, 4 March 1981, 77.
88. *LocalNet System 20 Overview*, Network Resources Corporation.
89. Kennett, D., 'UK gets broadband local network', *Computer Weekly*, 21 May 1981, 2.
90. Biba, K.J., 'Packet communication networks v. broadband coaxial cable', in *Local Network and Distributed Office Systems*, Online Publications, 1981, 611–625.
91. Lowe, L., 'LocalNet carries video, data traffic', *Electronics*, 30 June 1981, 139.
92. Kennett, D., 'Wang to use standard cable TV components in local network', *Computer Weekly*, 9 July 1981, 2.
93. *Videodata Broadband Communications Systems*, 3M United Kingdom.
94. Segarra, G., 'BIS—a broadband intercommunication system', in *Local Networks and Distributed Office Systems*, Online Publications, 1981, 185–198.
95. Christensen, G.S., 'Links between computer-room networks', *Telecommunications*, **13**, no.2, February 1979.
96. 'Critical eye', *Systems International*, February 1981, 33.
97. Thornton, J.E., 'Back-end network approaches', *Computer*, **13**, no.2, February 1980, 10.
98. Kennett, D., 'Massnet bridges mainframe gap', *Computer Weekly*, 23 April 1981, 4.
99. *Loosely Coupled Network (LCN)*, Control Data.
100. Iversen, W.R., 'CDC couples cpu's in fast network', *Electronics*, 30 June 1981.
101. Castueil, D.S., Giovachino, D.L., and Lengyel, D.L., 'The first all-in-one local network', *Data Communications*, August 1981, 93–102.
102. Electronic Newsletter, 'Local net offers 393 Mbps bandwidth', *Electronics*, 16 June 1982, 46–50.
103. Wilkin, D., 'Cable comparison', *Systems International*, August 1981.
104. 'Fibre optics overview', *Systems International*, August 1981.
105. Weissberger, A., 'Datalink controls and LSI circuits—the confluence of architecture and technology', *Computer Communications*, **1**, no.5, October 1978, 234–241.
106. Databreak, 'Broadband vs. baseband report', *Systems International*, May 1982, 10.
107. Faro, A. and Messina, G., 'Internetworking analysis', *Computer Communications*, **4**, no.4, August 1981, 169–173.
108. Beauchamp, K., 'Moving towards the "wired city" in computer communications', *Computer Weekly*, 23 July 1981, 16.

109. Elden, W. L., 'Gateways for interconnecting local area and long haul networks' in *Local Net and Distributed Office Systems*, Online Publications, 1981, 391–406.
110. Cerf, V. and Kahn, R., 'A protocol for packet network intercommunications', in *A Practical View Of Computer Communications Protocols*, IEEE Computer Society, 1978, 205–216.
111. Dallas, I.N., 'Implementation of a gateway between a Cambridge Ring local area network', in *Pathways to the Information Society*, Proceedings of the Sixth International Conference on Computer Communication, September 1982, 137–142.
112. Kennett, D., 'Local networks for satellite services', *Computer Weekly*, 19 March 1981.
113. Sunshine, C.A., 'Protocols for local networks', in *Local Networks and Distributed Office Systems*, Online Publications, l981, 245–261.
114. Treleaven, P.C. and Lima, I.G., 'Japan's fifth generation computer systems', *Computer*, August 1982, 79–88.
115. Treleaven, P.C., Hopkins, R.P., and Rautenbach, P.W., 'Combining data flows and control flow computing', *Computer Journal*, **25**, no.2, 1982, 207–217.
116. Treleaven, P.C., Brownbridge, D.R., and Hopkins, R.P., 'Data-driven and demand-driven computer architecture', *ACM Computing Surveys*, **14**, no.1, March 1982, 93–143.
117. *Local Area Networks*, Report to the Focus Committee, Department of Industry, UK.
118. Kennett, D., 'Net/One to be used in CASE local network', *Computer Weekly*, 19 March 1981.
119. Yeomans, J., 'The search for a single standard', *Computing*, 17 September 1981, 25.
120. 'Patent claims to hit net vendors', *Computing (Europe)*, 20 May 1982.
121. Kennett, D., 'More work needed on upper levels of ISO model', *Computer Weekly*, 19 March 1981.
122. Hindin, H.J., 'IBM to connect local networks', *Electronics*, 23 October 1980, 42.
123. Craver, D., 'Cambridge Ring boost', *Computer Weekly*, 13 August 1981.
124. Liebowitz, B.H., 'The dimensions of distributed processing', *Computer World/Extra*, 31 December 1980, 85.
125. Emery, F. and Trist, E., 'The causal texture of organizational environments', *Human Relations*, **18**, 1965, 21–32.
126. 'A new approach for local networks', *EDP Analyzer*, November 1981.
127. Burns, T. and Stalker, G., *The Management of Innovation*, Tavistock, London, 1961.
128. Pugh, D., Hickson, D., and Hinings, C., 'An empirical taxonomy of structures of work organizations', *Administrative Science Quarterly*, **14**, 1969.

129. Mintzberg, H., *The Structuring of Organizations*, Prentice-Hall, 1979.
130. Hiltz, R. and Turoff, H., 'The evolution of user behaviour in a computerized conferencing system', *Commun. ACM*, **24**, November 1981.
131. Olson, M., 'Remote office work—Implications for individuals and organizations', *CRIS Working Paper No.25*, GBA No.81–56(CR), New York University, 1981.
132. Craig, H., *Office Worker's Survival Handbook*, British Society for Social Responsibility in Science, 1981.
133. Cristie, B., *Face to File Communication*, Wiley, 1982.
134. Olson, M. and Lucas, H., 'The impact of office automation on the organization: Some implications for research and practice', *CRIS Working Paper No.1*, GBA No.80–46(CR), New York University, 1980.
135. Abraham, S., 'The impact of automated office systems on the productivity of managers and professionals', *1981 Office Automation Conference Digest*, AFIPS, 1981.
136. Lucas, H., *Why Information Systems Fail*, Columbia University Press, 1975.
137. Howard, N., 'A "cybernetic games" approach to OR 2', *OR Newsletter*, August 1981.
138. Owens, K., 'An on-line concept of implementation', *Systems, Objectives, Solutions*, **1**, no.2, April 1981.
139. Ginzberg, M., 'A prescriptive model of system implementation', *Systems, Objectives, Solutions*, **1**, no.1, January 1981.
140. Bostrom, R., 'A socio-technical perspective on MIS implementation', Paper presented at *ORSA/TIMS Conference*, November 1980.
141. Mumford, E., 'Participative systems design: structure and method', *Systems, Objectives, Solutions*, **1**, no.1, January 1981.
142. Hedberg, B., 'Using computerised information systems to design better organizations and jobs', in *The Human Side of Information Processing*, ed. N. Bjorn-Andersen, North-Holland, 1980.
143. Land, F., 'Notes on participation', *Computer Journal*, May 1982.
144. Sethi, N., 'A research model to study the environmental factors in management', *Management International Review*, **10**, 1970.
145. Lawrence, P., 'How to deal with resistance to change', *Harvard Business Review*, January-February 1969.
146. Hedberg, B., 'Computer systems to support industrial democracy', in *Human Choice and Computers*, vol.I, ed. H. Sackman, and E. Mumford, North-Holland, 1975.
147. Mumford, E. and Weir, M., *Computer Systems in Work Design—the ETHICS Method*, Associated Business Press, 1979.
148. Mumford, E., *'ETHICS'*, Participation Research Unit Paper, Manchester Business School, 1982.
149. Klein, H. and Hirschheim, R., 'Issues and approaches to appraising

technological change in the office: A consequentialist perspective', *ISRAM WP-8206-1.0*, June 1982.

150. Curley, K. and Pyburn, P., 'The evolution of intellectual technologies: reshaping the product life cycle?', *Working Paper HBS 80-31*, Harvard Business School, October 1980.

151. Bair, J., 'Experiences with an augmented human intellect system: computer mediated communication', *Proc. of Society for Information Display*, **14**, no.2, 1973, 42-51.

152. Gibson, R.W., 'Comparing features aids selecting broadband local net', *Data Communications*, April 1982, 127-135.

153. Viewpoint, 'The grim tale of a standards committee that has lost sight of its role and its importance', *Data Communications*, March 1982, 13.

154. Viewpoint, 'The IEEE 802 committee states its case concerning its local network standards efforts', *Data Communications*, April 1982, 13.

155. Newsfront, 'In sudden reversal IEEE embraces Ethernet', *Data Communications*, April 1982, 35-38.

156. Newsfront, 'IEEE group recasting its local net standard', *Data Communications*, March 1982, 42-44.

157. Clancy, G.J., 'A status report on the IEEE Project 802 local network standard', in *Local Networks and Distributed Office Systems*, Online Publications, 1981, 591-609.

158. Tanenbaum, A.S., 'Network protocols', *ACM Computing Surveys*, **13**, no.4., December 1981, 453-489.

159. Myers, W., 'Toward a local network standard', *IEEE Micro*, August 1982, 28-45.

160. Norton, J., Status report on IEEE Project 802, *ICCC 1982*, London, UK.

161. Sideris, G., 'World nears local-net standard', *Electronics*, 28 July 1982, 79-80.

162. Editorial, 'Have the 20 chosen the right standard', *Computing*, **10**, no.26, 1 July 1982, 13.

163. Rauch-Hindin, W., 'IBM's local network scheme', *Data Communications*, May 1982, 65-70.

164. Dataletter, '... As it tests voice/data token network', *Data Communications*, February 1982, 15.

165. Gardner, W.D., 'Solving the local network puzzle', *Datamation*, Special Report, 20 July 1982, 46-50.

166. Shoch, J.F. and Hupp, H.A., 'Measured performance of an Ethernet local network', *Commun.ACM.*, **23**, no.12, December 1980, 711.

167. Brotton, J., 'Fibre optic systems design', *Systems International*, July 1981, 40.

168. Zimmerman, H., 'OSI Reference Model—The ISO model of architecture for open systems interconnections', *IEEE Trans.Commun.*, **COM-28.4**, April 1980.

169. Hindin, H.J., 'Standards group play Ethernet down', *Electronics*, 3 July 1980.
170. *Hinet Computer Network*, Extel, UK
171. Spratt, E.B., 'Local area networks: management and quasi-political issues', in *Pathways to the Information Society*; Proceedings of the Sixth International Conference On Computer Communication, September 1982, 143–148.
172. *Introduction to DECnet*, Order No. AA-J055B-TK, Digital Software, January 1982.

Glossary

Address filtering: Same as 'Filter function'.

Asynchronous terminal: Those terminals that transmit on a character-by-character basis at data rates ranging from 50 to 300 bps.

Bandwidth: The range of frequencies available in any particular channel.

Baseband phase modulation: The modulation technique used on the Cambridge Ring over twisted pair wires where the signals along each pair of wires are out of phase by one bit time. Phase modulation allows a greater bandwidth to be employed by transmitting a clock pulse separately from the data. This reduces the bandwidth and introduces a direct current. However, twice the frequency has to be used as both the clock pulse and the data have to be transmitted.

Baseband signalling: Transmission of an unmodulated signal.

Basic block protocol (BBP): A protocol used on the Cambridge Ring which is responsible for transmitting blocks of data in minipackets from a source to its destination.

Baud: A unit of measure of the rate of modulation. Essentially, it is a unit of signal speed based on the number of changes in discrete events per second. Baud is equivalent to bits per second when each change in discrete events represents precisely one bit.

Binary countdown protocol: A contention-free protocol similar to the multilevel multiaccess protocol except binary addresses are used.

Bit map protocol: A protocol which implements a control strategy without any collisions occurring on the Ethernet. This is achieved by allocating a number of slots in the contention period. If a station wishes to transmit it will indicate this by setting a bit in its allocated slot. When the slots have passed, then the stations which have set a bit in their slot will begin transmitting in the order determined by the bit map, thus avoiding collisions.

Bit oriented protocol: These protocols are so-called because they allow packets to contain an arbitrary number of bits and are thus independent of the number of bits by which a character is represented. Thus, the packet size need not contain an integral number of bits that make up a character.

Braiding system: A system whereby secondary and tertiary cable paths are provided in addition to the main cable path. Such a system allows faulty devices or faulty cable units to be bypassed and hence not affect the rest of the system. A braiding system is employed on SILK.

Branching tree topology: The topology that results from interconnecting the nodes of a system in a geographically hierarchical manner. For example, one node may interconnect to distinct branches of the tree. On each branch one node may interconnect several smaller branches.

Bridge: Clark *et al.* [7] consider these devices which interconnect subnetworks to be intermediate in complexity between the multisegment repeaters and gateways. The interconnected subnetworks will use different media access protocols, but will employ the same addressing schemes. The bridge then will 'filter out' those addresses that do not belong to a subnetwork and retransmit it on the interconnected subnetwork according to that media access protocol.

Broadband signalling: The subdivision of the available bandwidth into discrete bands permitting the simultaneous transmission of multiple signals within these bands.

Broadcast communication: All messages transmitted on the communications subnetwork are theoretically received by all stations.

Buffer insertion: Synonymous with 'Register insertion'.

Bus interface unit (BIU): Dual Motorola 6809 microprocessor based interfaces used for attaching devices on Hyperbus.

Byte stream protocol (BSP): A Cambridge Ring protocol which determines courses of action that should be taken if a receiver station ignores a block of data, because an error has occurred or the receiver possesses no more buffer space. The BSP thus deals with those conditions that arise out of the BBP. Thus, the BSP uses sequence numbers, time-outs, and controls to ensure that transmitted data is in the correct sequence and in an error-free condition.

Cambridge Model Distributed System (CMDS): The distributed system implemented on the Cambridge Ring where a service similar to time-sharing is provided by allocating a user one of the available bank of computers for his sole use, instead of being allocated some share of a large computer.

Cambridge Ring: One of two main architectures for local area networks. In this approach, before a message can be sent from the sender station to the receiving station, the sender station must wait for a specific condition, e.g. empty slot, before it is allowed to transmit. Once this occurs, a message is transmitted and it travels in one direction passing each station on the ring until the receiving station is reached. The Cambridge Ring gets its name from two facts: (1) it was developed at the Computer Laboratory at Cambridge University, and (2) its topological structure is that of a ring.

CCITT: Comite Consultatif International Telegraphique et Telephonique is principally concerned with the interfaces to national networks, i.e. the user interface and the interface to networks of other countries, without concentrating on the characteristics of the network unless they affect the interfaces.

Channel: The medium which connects an entity sending a message with the entity receiving it.

Checksum word: Same as *'Cyclic redundancy checksum'*.

Circuit switching: A process whereby a connection is made between the sending entity and the receiving entity. Exclusive use of the circuit is given to the sending entity until the connection is released.

Circulating slot: A bit pattern which circulates around a ring and allows stations wishing to transmit to insert packets of fixed sizes into the slots.

Coaxial cable: Consists of a single central wire surrounded by a copper mesh and sometimes by an aluminium sheath, and then an insulating layer composed of Teflon or polyvinyl chloride (PVC). Coaxial cable can allow high data rates and is capable of supporting large bandwidths. The aluminium sheath version of coaxial cable is commonly used in the CATV industry, supporting bandwidths in excess of 300 MHz.

Collision window (also called 'Collision interval'): Same as *'Contention window/interval'*.

Concentric dielectric: The concentric dielectric is the medium which attempts to insulate the inner and outer cores of the coaxial cable from current flow. The medium could be air or it could be a special material with good insulating properties and thus the quality of the dielectric will ultimately effect the quality of the coaxial cable.

Contention: The situation which results from a number of units competing to use a limited resource. In the context of networks, this refers to a population of stations competing to use a shared resource—the communication subnetwork, e.g. the bus.

Contention-free protocol: A protocol implemented on a bus system which avoids collisions which result out of stations transmitting simultaneously.

Contention window (also called 'Contention interval'): This is the time interval between when a station senses the carrier free and thus transmits, and when it receives back its reflected transmission. This window has a maximum duration time equal to the time taken for a signal to be propagated along twice the length of the bus.

Control strategy: In the context of networks, the protocols or set of protocols implemented which allow stations on the network to share a resource, e.g. the subnetwork medium, so that transmission of data can take place over the network.

Control token: A bit pattern captured by a station which gives it permission to transmit. See *'Token passing'*.

Crossbar switch: Synonymous with *'Crosspoint switch'*.

Crosspoint switch: A method for sharing a number of memory modules among a number of processors. The crosspoint switch is essentially a matrix which allows each processor access to a number of memory modules.

CSMA: (See 'Ethernet')

CSMA-CD: (See 'Ethernet')

Cyclic redundancy checksum (CRC): A process performed on data to check for errors. The process involves dividing all serialized bits in a particular data block by a set binary number yielding a check character. The check character is then compared with some specified conditions to see if an error has occurred.

Daisy chaining: In communication systems, it refers to a cable or a line directly connecting a number of stations in a serial manner, as opposed to stations being connected to the line via interfaces or other devices in a parallel fashion.

Data circuit equipment (DCE): This is equipment which is provided by the PTT and terminates the PTT circuit on the user's premises and hence defines the boundary of the PTT network. An example of a DCE would be a modem.

Data terminal equipment (DTE): The user's equipment which is connected to a DCE. Thus, a DTE could range from a simple start-stop terminal to a mainframe computer.

Datagram service: A service which is provided in the network layer of the OSI reference model, which involves sending packets to a destination without reference to any other previous packet and which does not refer to any future packets. A datagram is often explained in terms of a telegram. They are analogous in that the delivery of both is not guaranteed and that there is no indication of whether delivery was successful.

DECnet: DEC's proprietary set of programs and protocols that allow two or more DEC computers to form a network. Every DECnet consists of software modules that perform DNA defined functions according to DNA defined rules.

Digital Network Architecture (DNA): The logical structure that provides an architecture for all DECnet implementations. DNA consists of nine layers— the communications facilities, physical link layer, data link layer, transport layer, network services layer, session control layer, network application layer, network management layer, and the user layer.

Direct memory access (DMA): A process which allows data to be transferred directly from memory without the normal intermediate stages of transfer to processor registers. This is normally done independently of the processor or via cycle-stealing.

Driver: In the context of communications, the driver usually means line driver. This is the hardware circuitry which is responsible for sending signals down the line.

DSC-3/4: Digital Microsystems series of Z80A based microcomputer systems.

Dual coaxial cable system: A communication system which employs two coaxial cables as the transmission medium.

Echoing support: The process of supporting echo checking. Here the received data in a transmission are 'echoed' back to the transmitting station so that the transmitting station can compare what was received with what was sent. In this way the accuracy of a transmission may be ascertained.

EIA: Electronic Industries Association is a US trade association for manufacturers of electronic products and which has a well developed standards department.

EPROM: Erasable programmable read only memories are ROMs which are programmable by a user.

Ether: The coaxial cable medium employed on the Ethernet. Ethernet is so-called because classical physicists considered that electromagnetic waves were propagated through a mystical ether.

Ethernet: The other of the two main architectures for local area networks. In this approach messages are broadcast along a passive medium (cable) from the sender station to the receiver station. To send a message, the sending station senses the cable to see if it is free. If it is free the station transmits, if it is occupied the station waits until it becomes free. This control strategy is referred to as carrier sense multiple access (CSMA). A variant of this strategy is when it senses the carrier free and transmits a station continues to sense the carrier to see that no other station transmitted at the same time. If this occurred, a collision between the two messages would have occurred thus precluding successful transmission. When this occurs, both stations stop transmitting and wait a random amount of time before attempting to retransmit. This is called carrier sense multiple access with collision detection (CSMA-CD). The Ethernet gets its name from the medium upon which transmission occurs, viz. the ether.

Fibre optics: Cables which are made from glass or plastic and can allow very high bandwidth, i.e. in excess of 3 GHz, with very low error rates. Fibre optics are not subject to electrical or electromagnetic interference.

Filter function: The function performed by a bridge in recognizing those addresses on packets which do not pertain to a subnetwork, but to another subnetwork. These packets are never addressed to the bridge but the bridge 'filters out' those packets with destination addresses located in other subnetworks.

Firmware: Usually referred to in the context of microprograms and is frequently applied to any resident program in a ROM. Thus, it cannot be altered. It is often thought of as an amalgamation of hardware and software.

Frequency agile modems: These are microprocessor based modems which are capable of modulating carrier waves of different frequencies in order to transmit data. Most modems are fixed frequency, i.e. they modulate a carrier wave of a fixed frequency.

Frequency division multiplexing (FDM): The process of dividing a transmission medium into a number of frequency bands, where each band is used as a communications channel.

Frequency shift keying (FSK): Also known as frequency modulation, where at least two frequencies (tones) are used to indicate the two bits 0 and 1. More than two tones could be used to indicate changes in bit patterns, i.e. 0 to 1, 1 to 0, 0 to 0, or 1 to 1.

Full duplex: A circuit which permits two-way simultaneous transmission.

Fully connected network: Where each node in the network is directly connected to every other node in the network.

Gateway: A switching exchange in one subnetwork through which access to another subnetwork is achieved. The gateway may perform addressing conversion and protocol conversions according to the differences between the two interconnected subnetworks.

Guard bands: A range of frequencies not used in the total bandwidth available for transmission in networks. These bandwidths separate the channels which are used for transmission purposes and prevent them from interfering with each other. Guard bands are used in satellite transmission and broadband LANs.

Half duplex: A circuit which permits two-way transmission, but at any one time in one direction only.

Hertz (Hz): A frequency measure equivalent to one cycle per second.

Hub polling: A process by which a central controlling device polls stations attached to a common bus. Usually the central controlling device polls the station at the extreme end of the bus. If this station has no message to transmit or is not ready for transmission, it passes the request to the next station. The request is passed on until a station transmits and then the controller will receive the message and forward it to the destination and resume polling the next station.

Institute of Electrical and Electronics Engineers (IEEE): The US body of professional engineers which publishes standards over a wide range of issues. In terms of LANs, the IEEE is attempting to produce standards under Project 802.

Interface: In the context of networking, a device which performs an intermediary function between an entity and the network.

International Organization for Standardization (ISO): The organization whose membership is made up by one standards group per nation. In the UK, the British Standards Institute is the member group. Subcommittee Sixteen

(SC16) is responsible for the Open System Interconnection (OSI) reference model.

Interrupt interface: A microprocessor based interface in which devices connected to the interface request services by interrupting the microprocessor. This is achieved by the attached devices sending a signal along an interrupt wire to the microprocessor.

Local blocks (LBL): These are the connection points to the network which handle register insertion for up to seven DCEs on SILK. The LBLs perform independent checks and transmit errors and faults to the main blocks (MBLs) of SILK. These functions are performed by a microprocessor based monitor in the LBL which uses test packets to diagnose failures.

Local circuit switched network (LCSN): A LAN that employs circuit switching technology to allow intercommunication amongst stations. Here, each station communicating with another does so over a dedicated circuit and hence each connection appears as a dedicated point-to-point link.

Local message switched network (LMSN): A local area network which employs message switching. Here the switching technology stores a message and determines its routing before retransmitting it. (See *'Store-and-forward'*.) Such a network could possess one or many switches of this nature.

Local non-switched network (LNSN): A LAN that employs no switching technology as all nodes are either completely interconnected or connected in a hierarchical manner that does not require switching technology.

Local packet switched network (LPSN): A local area network in which blocks of data or messages are divided up and transmitted as discrete packets.

LSI: Large-scale integration represents an approximate class of microprocessors where the equivalent of 100 to 10000 transistors per chip have been implemented.

LSI-11 bus: A DEC standard bidirectional asynchronous communication path between system components attached to the bus. This bus is common to all LSI-11 processors and peripherals. The bus provides vectored interrupts, programmed I/O transfers, and DMA I/O data transfers. The LSI-11 bus is a low end member of the DEC buses and possesses 42 bidirectional and two unidirectional lines which allow processor, memory, and I/O devices to communicate with each other.

Main blocks (MBL): These are similar to the local blocks used on SILK except for some additional features. These include bit timing synchronization, removing error packets which have not been removed by the destination, and certain test activities. There is typically one MBL per braid in any braided system.

MCZ-2: One of Zilog's series of Z80A based microcomputer systems.

Memory mapping: The hardware organization where both the main memory and all I/O ports communicate with the processor using a shared memory and I/O bus. Here each I/O port has an address in the main memory address space and an input or output port can respond to any instruction that accesses its address.

Modulation: A process whereby the characteristics of a carrier wave, i.e. the amplitude, frequency or phase, are altered by an impressed wave.

Mostek 6502: A standard microprocessor with an 8 bit wide data bus commonly used in personal computers.

Motorola 6809: A Motorola microprocessor with an 8 bit data bus, but has been regarded by some as a 16 bit microprocessor because its instruction set includes instructions with 16 bit opcodes.

MSI: Medium-scale integration is the approximate class of microprocessors where the equivalent of 10 to 100 transistors per chip have been implemented.

Multicore cable: A cable which is composed of many individual cables which would allow data to be transmitted in parallel or independently transmitted down each individual cable (see 'Space division multiplexing').

Multidrop line: When a number of devices (usually terminals) are connected to a single channel. Multidrop lines usually employ some type of polling process for the devices to transmit data. Multidrop lines are sometimes referred to as multipoint lines.

Multilevel multiaccess (MLMA): A contention-free protocol which allows stations to transmit according to their addresses. Essentially, this strategy allows those stations with the highest addresses to transmit first.

Multiplexing: A means of dividing up a transmission medium into multiple channels.

Multiported memory: A method for sharing memory among a population of processors. Each memory module has a number of ports, to which it is possible to connect a number of processors. Clearly, the number of processors that the memory modules can accommodate is limited by the number of ports.

Multisegment repeater: Referred to by Clark *et al*. [7] to be those devices which interconnect two subnetworks. These subnetworks will use the same packet formats, the same addressing schemes, and the same media access protocols and thus their function is primarily to recognize addresses that do not belong to one subnetwork and to transmit the packet on another subnetwork.

Multistation intercommunication unit (MSIU): A device which allows up to four computers and/or terminals (DTEs) to attach to the Philips Intercommunication Pipe (PHIP).

Network access device (NAD): The interface device which allows processors or peripherals to connect to the LAN product Loosely Coupled Network (LCN). The NAD accesses the coaxial cable by a 'self-synchronizing, rotating priority protocol', i.e. a TDM technique without centralized control sometimes referred to as virtual token passing. The NAD also performs buffer allocation, message flow, error recovery and logging, and conversion.

Network interface unit (NIU): The programmable interfaces based on the Z80A microprocessor used to attach devices on Net/One. There are essentially two parts to the NIU—the transmitter/receiver and a network processor, which performs the low-level communications protocol and provides an intelligent interface for the attached device.

Orbital Test Satellite (OTS): A European Communities satellite operating at a data transmission rate of 1 to 2 Mbps and requiring a 3 m reception disk.

OSI Reference Model: The Open System Interconnection Reference Model is a seven-layered architecture for communication drawn up by ISO/TC97/SC16. The concept of the 'open' communication system is one in which a user may communicate with another user without being constrained by the equipment of a particular manufacturer.

The OSI Reference Model has seven layers. These are the physical, data link, network, transport, session, presentation, and application layers.

The function of the physical layer, which is the lowest layer in the architecture, is concerned with the mechanical and electrical characteristics of transmitting data over the physical medium of the communication subnetwork, but is not concerned with the significance or meaning of the bits.

The data link layer is responsible for taking the transmission provided by the physical layer and transforming it into an error-free line. This is achieved by decomposing the input data into manageable units and adding flow control and error correction to the basic physical layer service.

The function of the network layer is the routing, addressing, relaying, and flow control of packets through the subnetwork and provides services of varying quality to the layer above. All layers higher than the network layers have end-to-end connections but if concatenation through a number of different subnetworks is involved, the relay function of the network layer may enhance the service of those lower-quality networks so that the overall connection is improved.

The transport layer performs a function which is network independent and is responsible for data transfer between the two communicating hosts (end-to-end) by optimizing the use of the available network connections.

The session layer establishes a connection and manages the interchange between the user and a process on another machine in an orderly manner.

The presentation layer manipulates the data for presentation to the application layer so that applications may exchange information, irrespective of each application's representation of that information, e.g. different character codes, encryption, and compression.

The uppermost layer is the application layer where the user determines which services to use so that communication can take place between the application processes. Although the services that could be provided by this layer can vary greatly, there is some commonality in that data transfer between application processes would also involve some determination of the availability of the destination, authorization, privacy, data integrity, error control, and the assessment of the available resources.

The architecture that a model like the OSI Reference Model presents is necessitated because of the complex nature of computer networks. The organization of a network into distinct layers allows each layer to be assigned a different task, but the basic task is essentially the transfer of information to the next layer above and the OSI Reference Model furnishes the basis for defining communication standards, but makes no attempt actually to specify the services and the protocols.

PABX (Private Automatic Branch Exchange): Traditionally, a switch used in organizations for the routing of telephone messages.

Packet: A formatted group of bits containing both data and control information which is sent along the transmission medium as a collective unit.

Packet assembly/disassembly (PAD): A PAD allows start-stop character mode terminals to exchange data with packet mode terminals over a packet switched network. The PAD functions by accepting data from the start-stop terminal and assembling it into packets and then transmitting the packet to the packet mode terminal. It also performs the reverse process of accepting packets from the packet mode terminal and transmitting them to the start-stop terminal. CCITT recommendation X.3 defines the PAD functions, X.28 specifies the protocol between the PAD and the start-stop terminal and X.29 specifies the protocol between a PAD and a packet mode terminal, i.e. a DTE.

Packet switching: The process of transmitting packets of data from sender to receiver where the transmission channel is only occupied for the period of time while the packet is being transmitted.

Permanent virtual circuit (PVC): A private circuit established over a packet switched network, which is set up once and never terminated, thus allowing data packets to be transmitted only.

Phase-locked loop: Where a reference signal is compared with a frequency of a voltage-controlled oscillator. The difference between the two frequencies will then be output as direct current and re-input, after amplification, and will drive the voltage-controlled oscillator towards the reference frequency. This will result in the voltage-controlled oscillator being synchronized with the incoming reference frequency. A phase-locked loop is used on the Cambridge Ring as a clocking mechanism. As the bits are encoded to provide a pulse with each bit sent, these can be decoded and input to the phase-locked loop, as a synchronization method.

Philips Intercommunication Pipe (PHIP): A 4 Mbps channel in the LAN product BIS which allows up to 1024 different devices to be connected.

Point-to-point connection: A connection between two entities without the intervention of an intermediate device.

Polling: The sequential process of inviting entities to transmit data.

Program interrupt interface unit: An interrupt interface provided for devices attached to Polynet.

Protocol: A set of rules which govern the format and synchronization of message interchange between two communicating entities.

PTT (Post, Telephone, and Telegraph Authority): A governmental body which provides general communications services in most parts of the world with the exception of North America.

Q-bus: Synonymous with 'LSI-11 bus'.

RAM: Random access memory is memory which allows data to be written to and read from.

Register insertion: A media access method where a packet is first placed in a shift register which is then inserted onto the network when the network becomes free.

Remote host facility (RHF): Software provided for the LAN product LCN which controls the transfer of information between computers. The procedures associated with the RHF include transfer of permanent files, transfer of jobs and output files, and application-to-application interaction.

ROM: Read only memory is a memory which can only be read from. It is usually programmed by the manufacturer, and once programmed it is not normally changed.

RS232C: An EIA standard that defines the electric signal characteristics and connector pin assignments for the interchange of serial binary data between a DTE and DCE, e.g. minicomputers to modems.

RS422: An EIA integrated circuit compatible standard that defines an interface circuit for high-speed binary data interchange, providing greater immunity to noise and giving lower error rates.

S-100 bus: A common 100 wire bus in which some of the wires have standard operations defined on them.

Screen: Materials, usually of a bounded nature, used to provide insulation for a cable or media. Examples are Teflon and polyvinyl chloride (PVC).

SDLC: Synchronous data link control is a bit oriented data link protocol used in IBM's System Network Architecture (SNA).

Shared memory system: The class of system in which a population of processors, usually separated by a few metres, interact by accessing a common memory.

Shift register: A register in which a packet is placed prior to transmission.

Single shot protocol (SSP): A protocol used on the Cambridge Ring for making requests to the name server for down line loading. In this sense, the protocol is transaction oriented, i.e. it requests data to be supplied and then receives the data back.

Slave unit: A unit or device which is subordinate to another which is called a master. In the context of communications, the slave is subordinate to the master in that the former is instructed and controlled by the latter and told when it is allowed to transmit.

Space division multiplexing (SDM): A means to increase the number of channels available for transmission by adding additional transmission cables.

SSI: Small-scale integration represents the approximate class of microprocessors where the equivalent of up to 10 transistors have been implemented on a single chip.

Star configuration: The topology that results from devices being connected to a central primary node alone. There is no interconnection between the devices except through the central node.

Store-and-forward: The handling of messages on a network in such a fashion that messages are accepted— and stored if necessary—by the network and then passed on to the receiving entity.

Switching technology: In the context of communications, it is those systems that employ technology that allows the desired switching of circuits, messages, and/or packets.

Synchronous terminals: Those terminals that transmit in synchronous mode, i.e. relying on a fixed time interval for message exchange (often considered as an alternative to character-by-character exchange). These terminals usually operate at data rates ranging from 600 to 48000 bps.

System Network Architecture (SNA): IBM's proprietary network architecture which allows IBM products to build their own networks in a coherent manner. The architecture has six layers—the physical link control, the data link control, path control, transmission control, data flow control, network addressable services, and end user.

Tbox: The tap which connects devices to the coaxial cable in LocalNet.

Time division multiplexing (TDM): The process of dividing a transmission medium into a number of channels, where different channels operate over the medium at different times.

Time-shared bus: A bus system to which stations are attached and on which the control strategy employed allows each station to use the bus for a predetermined period of time.

Timing tolerance: The modulation and clocking scheme, referred to in the context of the Cambridge Ring, which allows each bit to be clearly defined. (See Hopper [24] for an extended treatment on this subject.)

Token passing: A bit pattern which is captured by a station prior to transmission of a variable size packet. After transmission the station releases the token which is seized by any station wishing to transmit.

Topology: The structure which results from the manner in which entities are interconnected.

Transport protocols: Those protocols in the transport layer of the OSI Reference Model. The transport protocol provides those services which are not provided by the services available and facilities desired. The functions of the transport layer can thus be very complex depending on the reliability of the underlying subnetwork. Essentially, the transport protocol is responsible for host-to-host communication across the entire network.

Transporter: The name given to the interfaces for microcomputers and minicomputers of Corvus System's LAN product Omninet. The transporter is so-called because it is claimed that it implements the first four layers of the ISO OSI reference model, i.e. the physical, data link, network, and transport layers.

Transmission medium: The physical channel which provides the means of interconnection between two nodes on a network. Transmission media can be bounded, e.g. coaxial cable, fibre optics, twisted copper pairs, or unbounded, e.g. radio waves over the air.

Tree walk protocol: A limited contention protocol in which all stations are allowed to compete for the first available contention window on a carrier sense network. If a collision occurs during this first contention interval, then automatically a group of stations are eliminated from contending during the next window. Similarly if a collision occurs again, another subset of stations is eliminated and contention will only occur between those remaining stations. Hence, this protocol can be structured like a tree and when traffic is heavy and the number of collisions are high, the search for a station will begin further down the tree.

Twisted pair: Copper wires are twisted to prevent the many pairs of wires from interfering with the transmissions on each other. Twisted pairs are extensively used for local telephone connections.

Uncommitted logic array (ULA): Essentially a ULA is a custom designed chip in which a range of standard chips contains an array of logic gates which are complete in themselves, but are not interconnected in any particular circuit pattern. The computer then converts a logic diagram which may have been composed by a customer and the arrays can be interconnected to achieve the required pattern. Such ULA chips have been made by Ferranti with two chips—hence the term 'ULA 2 chip'.

UNET: This is the software communications product offered by 3COM for machines running the UNIX operating system. UNET uses the internet protocol and the transmission control protocol developed by the Defense Advanced Research Projects Agency in the US and its features include remote file transfer, virtual terminal facilities, process-to-process communications, electronic mail transfer, and datagram service.

Unibus: A DEC standard asynchronous bidirectional bus to which medium- and low-speed peripheral devices are attached to the cpu. Originally developed for the PDP-11, it was extended to the VAX. There are 56 lines on the Unibus communication path that links I/O devices to a Unibus adaptor which is part of the cpu. The Unibus adaptor performs priority arbitration among Unibus devices and performs the necessary translation of addresses, data, and control information that passes along the Unibus lines. During any bus operation one device, the bus master, controls the bus when communicating with another device on the bus, which acts as a slave.

UNIX: The operating system developed by Bell Laboratories.

Urn protocol: A limited contention protocol in which an urn is viewed as containing green balls and red balls. The former represent those stations that are ready to transmit and the latter those stations not. Here a window of certain size (number of stations) allows those stations in the window to contend. If a collision occurs then the window size is reduced but if a successful transmission results, the window moves to another group of stations. The urn protocol is so called because in each window there is a probability of some stations wanting to transmit simultaneously, i.e. drawing two green balls out of the urn without replacement.

V.24: A CCITT recommendation which lists definitions of interchange circuits between DTEs and DCEs. It is not a full interface specification, but does define DTE/DCE interfaces in terms of physical connectors, interchange circuits, and the operational requirements of the interchange circuits, all conforming to CCITT modem recommendations. V.24 is almost identical to RS232C except for small differences in the interchange circuits and certain pin allocations in the physical connector.

Virtual circuit: A network layer service in which the sequence of packets sets up a call, allows the exchange of data to occur, and then terminates the call over a packet switched network. The call is 'virtual' because the channel or transmission capacity is not exclusively reserved for that call, but the network is still aware that the call exists.

VLSI: Very large-scale integration represents an approximate class of microprocessors where the equivalent of over 10000 transistors on a chip have been implemented.

Wide area network (WAN): A term which includes those networks that span large or considerable distances, often on a national or international basis. Traditionally, they could not provide the high data rates that LANs could offer, but this is changing with the use of fibre optics and satellite technology. The major distinction between WANs and LANs is the protocols employed to access the network. For instance, the propagation delay makes the use of CSMA-CD implausible on a satellite link or a national fibre optic link. Cambridge Ring technology could not be used as WANs do not usually have a ring topology. Further, protocols are usually more complicated in WANs because of the higher error rates that occur.

XLR plug: Similar to a five-pin DIN plug. This plug and socket connection is used on Polynet.

X.21: A CCITT physical layer protocol that specifies the characteristics of a general purpose digital interface between a DTE and a DCE for synchronous operation on public data networks.

X.25: A collective CCITT recommendation for the protocol of the physical, data link, and network layers of the OSI Reference Model. It specifies the protocols for packet mode terminals which would be capable of supporting several virtual circuits, permanent virtual circuits or for datagram service.

X.75: A CCITT recommendation for an internetworking protocol which builds on the X.25 protocol, defining the signalling system between two packet switched networks.

Index

190